AMERICAN
WAR LIBRARY

★ ★ ★ ★

★ Vietnam War ★

Primary Sources

Edited by David M. Haugen

LUCENT BOOKS
SAN DIEGO, CALIFORNIA

THOMSON
★
™
GALE

Detroit • New York • San Diego • San Francisco
Boston • New Haven, Conn. • Waterville, Maine
London • Munich

Titles in the American War Library series include:

World War I
Flying Aces
Leaders and Generals
Life in the Trenches
Strategic Battles
Weapons of War

World War II
Hitler and the Nazis
Kamikazes
Leaders and Generals
Life as a POW
Life of an American Soldier in
  Europe

Strategic Battles in Europe
Strategic Battles in the Pacific
The War at Home
Weapons of War

The Civil War
Leaders of the North and
  South
Life Among the Soldiers and
  Cavalry
Lincoln and the Abolition of
  Slavery
Strategic Battles
Weapons of War

Library of Congress Cataloging-in-Publication Data

Primary sources / edited by David M. Haugen.
      p. cm. — (American war library. Vietnam War)
Includes bibliographical references and index.
Summary: Presents the original documents used as source material for
the American War Library, Vietnam War series.
  ISBN 1-59018-203-0 (alk. paper)
  1. Vietnamese conflict, 1961–1975—Sources—Juvenile literature. [1.
Vietnamese Conflict, 1961–1975—Sources.]
I. Haugen, David M., II. Series.
  DS557.4 .TP75 2002
  959.704'3—dc21

2001007310

✦ Contents ✦

A Nation Forged by War

he United States, like many nations, was forged and defined by war. Despite Benjamin Franklin's opinion that "There never was a good war or a bad peace," the United States owes its very existence to the War of Independence, one to which Franklin wholeheartedly subscribed. The country forged by war in 1776 was tempered and made stronger by the Civil War in the 1860s.

The Texas Revolution, the Mexican-American War, and the Spanish-American War expanded the country's borders and gave it overseas possessions. These wars made the United States a world power, but this status came with a price, as the nation became a key but reluctant player in both World War I and World War II.

Each successive war further defined the country's role on the world stage. Following World War II, U.S. foreign policy redefined itself to focus on the role of defender, not only of the freedom of its own citizens, but also of the freedom of people everywhere. During the cold war that followed World War II until the collapse of the Soviet Union, defending the world meant fighting communism. This goal, manifested in the Korean and Vietnam conflicts, proved elusive, and soured the American public on its achievability. As the United States emerged as the world's sole superpower, American foreign policy has been guided less by national interest and more on protecting international human rights. But as involvement in Somalia and Kosovo prove, this goal has been equally elusive.

As a result, the country's view of itself changed. Bolstered by victories in World Wars I and II, Americans first relished the role of protector. But, as war followed war in a seemingly endless procession, Americans began to doubt their leaders, their motives, and themselves. The Vietnam War especially caused people to question the validity of sending its young people to die in places where they were not particularly wanted and for people who did not seem especially grateful.

While the most obvious changes brought about by America's wars have been geopolitical in nature, many other aspects of society have been touched. War often does not bring about change directly, but acts instead like the catalyst in a chemical reaction, accelerating changes already in progress.

Some of these changes have been societal. The role of women in the United States had been slowly changing, but World War II put thousands into the workforce and into uniform. They might have gone back to being housewives after the war, but equality, once experienced, would not be forgotten.

Likewise, wars have accelerated technological change. The necessity for faster airplanes and a more destructive bomb led to the development of jet planes and nuclear energy. Artificial fibers developed for parachutes in the 1940s were used in the clothing of the 1950s.

Lucent Books' American War Library covers key wars in the development of the nation. Each war is covered in several volumes, to allow for more detail, context, and to provide volumes on often neglected subjects, such as the kamikazes of World War II, or weapons used in the Civil War. As with all Lucent Books, notes, annotated bibliographies, and appendixes such as glossaries give students a launching point for further research. In addition, sidebars and archival photographs enhance the text. Together, each volume in The American War Library will aid students in understanding how America's wars have shaped and changed its politics, economics, and society.

Chapter 1

Entering the War

In 1954, France lost control over its colony of Vietnam. For nearly a decade French soldiers had been fighting the Vietminh, revolutionary forces within Vietnam that sought national independence. The Vietminh were a Communist-led peasant army, but their guerrilla warfare tactics drained the French military of its will to fight and the French government of its financial capacity to wage a war that it seemingly could not win. After a humiliating defeat at the battle of Dien Bien Phu, France decided to bring the costly conflict to a close. As part of the peace accords, Vietnam was temporarily partitioned into the Communist North and a democratic South—with a nationwide election to be held in 1956 that would unite the country under one government.

The United States, under presidents Harry S. Truman and subsequently Dwight D. Eisenhower, had supported the French in their bid to retain their colony. Since the end of World War II the United States had been embroiled in a cold war with the Soviet Union, and the government feared the loss of Vietnam to Communist forces. As the French began withdrawing from Vietnam, America was faced with a decision: allow the general election to take place and risk another Communist republic in Southeast Asia or intervene on the behalf of the South Vietnamese government and resist the possible Communist takeover. The choice, however, seemed preordained. Just prior to Dien Bien Phu, President Eisenhower had held a press conference and explained that America's duty was to stop the spread of communism in Southeast Asia. If Vietnam fell to the Communists, the president argued, other nations in the region would succumb in short order. After the French surrender, the United States was compelled to act.

Although Eisenhower's sentiments were echoed by his successor, John F. Kennedy, neither president was willing to use U.S. military might in Vietnam. America

French and Vietnamese prisoners of the Vietminh march from the battlefields after defeat at Dien Bien Phu.

already had military advisors in Vietnam, ostensibly training the South Vietnamese Army (ARVN) to defend its borders. Through 1961, Kennedy increased the number of advisors and put U.S. special forces in the region to carry out covert operations against the North Vietnamese military. The United States was also by then supplying the South Vietnamese with weapons and munitions to sustain its fight. The overall hope was that by strengthening the ARVN, American troops might not be drawn into the conflict.

The hope was in vain. A report from a special delegation sent to South Vietnam indicated that South Vietnam's army was in shambles and that the leadership of President Ngo Dinh Diem was ineffectual at best and tyrannical at worst. Kennedy had to come up with a new plan. Unfortunately, in November of 1963, Kennedy was assassinated. The choice of possibly escalating America's involvement fell to President Lyndon B. Johnson.

Johnson faced a much more desperate situation in South Vietnam. The same month of Kennedy's assassination, President Diem had been captured and executed by a military coup. But the government remained in flux as three more South Vietnamese leaders would come and go in a matter of months. Although South Vietnam's government appeared unstable, Johnson reaffirmed America's support for the nation. In August 1964, America's pledge of commitment was tested. At the beginning of the month, two U.S. warships in the Gulf of Tonkin reported that they had been fired upon by North Vietnamese vessels while in international waters. Whether the Johnson administration trumped up this incident to force the nation to act is still a subject of controversy. Regardless, the president asked Congress to empower him with the ability to protect U.S. interests in Vietnam by "all necessary measures." Congress agreed, and America was propelled into the hostilities.

Without a formal declaration of war, Johnson ordered U.S. warplanes to begin a bombing campaign against North Vietnam in February 1965. A month later, 3,500 U.S. Marines landed at Da Nang in South Vietnam to begin fighting North Vietnamese regulars and their Viet Cong counterparts in the South. America had now become committed to waging a ground war in Vietnam, a war that its ally France could not win a decade earlier. And it would be another long, agonizing decade before the United States learned the same lesson the French had.

U.S. Aid Has Not Helped South Vietnam

Between 1954 and 1957, British journalist David Hotham worked in Saigon as a foreign correspondent for British and American newspapers and magazines. In this 1957 article from the American journal New Republic, *Hotham criticizes the aid program the United States set up to support the republic of South Vietnam. According to Hotham, the bulk of American financial support is being misspent. No money is reaching the Vietnamese peasants who badly need it. Instead U.S. aid is being hoarded by the regime of President Ngo Dinh Diem to finance the South Vietnamese army. Hotham views this misguided effort as indicative of American foreign policy in Vietnam.*

The present writer spent nearly three years in Saigon as the correspondent of an English newspaper. He has no axe to grind other than to make what contribution he can to the over-riding objective of saving the people of this corner of Asia from the desperate system of Communism. It is his view that Western policy in South Vietnam has gone completely off the rails, and unless it is radically changed *now*, will utterly fail in its main objectives. If South Vietnam goes Communist, or is again plunged in chaos, it will be a dangerous shock for the Western world and a menace for the rest of Asia. Such, however, is the danger today, and the Western nation mainly concerned is the United States.

Into this little country of 11 million inhabitants the US has pumped about $770 million of aid since the end of the Indo-China War in 1954. It has given the government of President Ngo Dinh Diem every kind of support that a great power can give to a small—diplomatic, military, economic, moral. Yet, it has to be admitted, and the Americans themselves do admit it, that those who bring this unstinting aid are not liked in the country to which they bring it, and that the economic situation there, instead of improving as the result of it, is rapidly deteriorating. What is wrong?

When the Indo-China War was lost the best hope of saving the South from Communism depended on three main objectives of Western policy being achieved—and achieved with the least possible delay. These were: *first,* to unite South Vietnam under a political leadership which had a popular basis among its own people; *second,* to give the South genuine political and economic independence so that it could stand up against, and indeed outbid, Communist North Vietnam in this respect; *third,* a more long-term, but perhaps even more important objective than the other two, to lift the standard of living of the Asian masses south of the 17th parallel at a speed greater than those masses might suppose that Communism could do it for them. The fulfillment of these three objectives within a measurable period was the precondition of a victory for the West in what was left to them of Indo-China. Despite the massive aid program none of

these objectives have been achieved. They have hardly even been tried. . . .

US aid has been generous. But how has it been spent? 64 percent of the $770 million poured into the little country since 1954 has been used simply to pay the wages of the 150,000-strong army. . . .

The upshot is that more than four-fifths of the whole gigantic aid program has failed to contribute in any direct way to the well-being of the Southern population, which should of course have been the primary objective since the beginning. None of it has been used to cure the growing unemployment. Almost none has been used to build houses for the people. Not a single industry has been created in the South since the end of the Indo-China War. The Southern population, which knows well enough what large sums have been spent in its country, knows equally well that almost none of this money has come its way. This not only breeds hatred of the West, it contradicts the whole principle of Western aid to "backward" countries—the principle of preventing Communism by improving the lot of most of the people. . . .

It is easy to be critical; it is less easy to be constructive. But in this case what ought to be done sticks out a mile. It is to take the original principles of policy out of the pigeon-holes, dust them off, and then simply *apply* them. To unite the South, all the anti-Communist elements available in the country should be brought in to help the running of the country, instead of being kept out. It is painful to see so many able men kicking their heels in idleness and frustration in South Vietnam. Secondly, the aid program should be recast (whether or not the volume of aid is cut) so that it aims at making South Vietnam economically independent of the US within the shortest time possible. At the same time, the total amount of the aid should be spent on improving the living standards of the people who live in the country to whom it is given, and not on anything else. . . .

A final point may be added. If President Ngo Dinh Diem objects to such a change in policy, the West should remember that South Vietnam is *not* in fact economically independent today. Pressure can and should be used. Gross mistakes have been made in South Vietnam. The Western policymakers should realize that the whole aim and object of their policy is not merely to keep one particular man or group of men in power. It is to live up to their declared principles. If they do not act now, it will be too late. They will have done permanent harm to their future in Asia.

David Hotham, "South Vietnam—Shake Bastion," *New Republic*, November 25, 1957.

"America's Stake in Vietnam"

In 1956, then-senator John F. Kennedy established his position on America's support of the government of South Vietnam. Speaking to the American Friends of Vietnam, a lobbying group that backed South Vietnamese president Ngo Dinh Diem and a free South Vietnam, Kennedy declares that the United States has an important stake in the fate of South Vietnam. America must prove its resolve to offer alternatives to the Communist influences in Southeast Asia or suffer a loss of prestige and national security. Kennedy had previously cautioned against U.S. military commitment in Vietnam, but in this address he acknowledges the potential that force may be needed to ensure American interests are preserved.

Let us briefly consider exactly what is "America's Stake in Vietnam":

(1) *First,* Vietnam represents the cornerstone of the Free World in Southeast Asia, the keystone to the arch, the finger in the dike. Burma, Thailand, India, Japan, the Philippines and obviously Laos and Cambodia are among those whose security would be threatened if the red tide of Communism overflowed into Vietnam. . . .

(2) *Secondly,* Vietnam represents a proving ground of democracy in Asia. However we may choose to ignore it or deprecate it, the rising prestige and influence of Communist China in Asia are unchallengeable facts. Vietnam represents the alternative to Communist dictatorship. If this democratic experiment fails, if some one million refugees have fled the totalitarianism of the North only to find neither freedom nor security in the South, then weakness, not strength, will characterize the meaning of democracy in the minds of still more Asians. . . .

(3) *Third* and in somewhat similar fashion, Vietnam represents a test of American responsibility and determination in Asia. If we are not the parents of little Vietnam, then surely we are the godparents. We presided at its birth, we gave assistance to its life, we have helped to shape its future. As French influence in the political, economic and military spheres has declined in Vietnam, American influence has steadily grown. This is our offspring—we cannot abandon it, we cannot ignore its needs. And if it falls victim to any of the perils that

While still a senator, John F. Kennedy asserts the importance of American involvement in fighting communism in Vietnam.

threaten its existence—Communism, political anarchy, poverty and the rest—then the United States, with some justification, will be held responsible; and our prestige in Asia will sink to a new low.

(4) *Fourth* and finally, America's stake in Vietnam, in her strength and in her security, is a very selfish one—for it can be measured, in the last analysis, in terms of

American lives and American dollars. It is now well known that we were at one time on the brink of war in Indo-China—a war which could well have been more costly, more exhausting and less conclusive than any war we have ever known. The threat of such war is not now altogether removed from the horizon. Military weakness, political instability or economic failure in the new state of Vietnam could change almost overnight the apparent security which has increasingly characterized that area under the leadership of President Diem. And the key position of Vietnam in Southeast Asia, as already discussed, makes inevitable the involvement of this nation's security in any new outbreak of trouble.

John F. Kennedy, Address to the American Friends of Vietnam, June 1956.

The United States Should Commit to South Vietnam

By the time John F. Kennedy became president of the United States, the government of South Vietnam was embroiled in a war against Communist insurgent forces within its borders. To bolster the South Vietnamese military, Kennedy increased the sale of weaponry (from handheld armaments to helicopters and tanks) to South Vietnam. He also provided South Vietnam with additional American military advisors who went into the field with Army of the Republic of Vietnam (ARVN)

troops. In this cabinet report from November 1961, Kennedy's secretary of defense, Robert S. McNamara, and secretary of state, Dean Rusk, strongly suggest that more than military hardware will be needed in saving South Vietnam. The two advisors agree that the United States should do everything in its power to stop the spread of communism in Vietnam—including sending U.S. combat troops into the troubled nation.

United States National Interests in South Viet-Nam.

The deteriorating situation in South Viet-Nam requires attention to the nature and scope of United States national interests in that country. The loss of South Viet-Nam to Communism would involve the transfer of a nation of 20 million people from the free world to the Communism bloc. The loss of South Viet-Nam would make pointless any further discussion about the importance of Southeast Asia to the free world; we would have to face the near certainty that the remainder of Southeast Asia and Indonesia would move to a complete accommodation with Communism, if not formal incorporation with the Communist bloc. The United States, as a member of SEATO [Southeast Asia Treaty Organization], has commitments with respect to South Viet-Nam under the Protocol to the SEATO Treaty. Additionally, in a formal statement at the conclusion session of the 1954 Geneva Conference, the United States representative stated that the United States "would view any renewal of the aggression . . . with grave concern and seriously threatening international peace and security."

The loss of South Viet-Nam to Communism would not only destroy SEATO but would undermine the credibility of American commitments elsewhere. Further, loss of South Viet-Nam would stimulate bitter domestic controversies in the United States and would be seized upon by extreme elements to divide the country and harass the Administration. . . .

The United States' Objective in South Viet-Nam.

The United States should commit itself to the clear objective of preventing the fall of South Viet-Nam to Communism. The basic means for accomplishing this objective must be to put the Government of South Viet-Nam [GVN] into a position to win its own war against the Guerrillas. We must insist that that Government itself take the measures necessary for that purpose in exchange for large-scale United States assistance in the military, economic and political fields. At the same time we must recognize that it will probably not be possible for the GVN to win this war as long as the flow of men and supplies from North Viet-Nam continues unchecked and the guerrillas enjoy a safe sanctuary in neighboring territory.

We should be prepared to introduce United States combat forces if that should become necessary for success. Dependent upon the circumstances, it may also be necessary for United States forces to strike at the source of the aggression in North Viet-Nam. . . .

In the light of the foregoing, the Secretary of State and the Secretary of Defense recommend that:

1. We now take the decision to commit ourselves to the objective of preventing the fall of South Viet-Nam to Communism and that, in doing so, we recognize that the introduction of United States and other SEATO forces may be necessary to achieve this objective. (However, if it is necessary to commit outside forces to achieve the foregoing objective our decision to introduce United States forces should not be contingent upon unanimous SEATO agreement thereto.)

2. The Department of Defense be prepared with plans for the use of United States forces in South Viet-Nam under one or more of the following purposes:

(a) Use of a significant number of United States forces to signify United States determination to defend Viet-Nam and to boost South Viet-Nam morale.

(b) Use of substantial United States forces to assist in suppressing Viet Cong insurgency short of engaging in detailed counter-guerrilla operations but including relevant operations in North Viet-Nam.

(c) Use of United States forces to deal with the situation if there is organized Communist military intervention.

Dean Rusk and Robert S. McNamara, Report to President Kennedy, November 11, 1961.

South Vietnam Is Winning the War Against Communism

During the early years of U.S. involvement in Vietnam, media attention seemed to reinforce the optimism of government officials. With U.S. backing and the support of military advisors, the government of Ngo Dinh Diem was cast as winning the war against communism in South Vietnam. An article from Time *magazine in 1962 reflects this rosy outlook as it follows two U.S. generals, Maxwell Taylor and Paul Harkins, during their inspection of South Vietnam's military forces. While the* Time *article notes the military improvements in the struggling nation, it is critical of the despotic tendencies of Diem's regime—a potential problem for the eagerly anticipated "social revolution" in South Vietnam.*

Over rutted jungle roads and through remote mountain villages, General Maxwell D. Taylor Jeeped and walked last week on a

Vietnamese villagers line up for inspection by U.S. generals Maxwell Taylor and Paul Harkins.

first-hand inspection tour of South Viet Nam's hard, ugly war against the Communist Viet Cong. Taylor, who takes over as chairman of the Joint Chiefs of Staff next month, last visited Viet Nam a year ago; from that trip came the stepped-up program of U.S. military and economic aid to the embattled nation. Last week, in talks with President Ngo Dinh Diem and General Paul Harkins, boss of U.S. forces in Viet Nam, hard-bitten Maxwell Taylor sought to assess the results. His conclusion: "We are making progress."

Since last October, the U.S. has boosted its force of military advisers to more than 10,000, and is now spending $1,000,000 daily to beat the Viet Cong. This year the U.S. will help arm some 130,000 members of the Civil Guard and the Self-Defense Corps, and train them both to defend their villages and to make short-range thrusts against the Viet Cong. The regular army will be boosted from seven to nine divisions, with a total force of 200,000 men; U.S.-backed training programs will also double the size of the army's officer and NCO corps.

With the growth of the militiamen, the army is being released from static holding operations to make major offensive sweeps against the Viet Cong, sometimes clearing them from areas where no government forces have been in 15 years. In Kien Phong and Vinh Long provinces, where the Reds once dominated up to 65% of the population, swiftly mounted government raids against guerrilla training centers and sup-

ply depots have reduced the Communist-controlled populace to less than 30%. . . .

But the country is under considerable and mounting strain.

Politically, despite the pleadings of U.S. officials—and rumbles of discontent from his opponents—Diem is in no mood to relax his authoritarian rule. Economically, the war has taken a heavy toll. The Viet Cong have cut off rice shipments from the interior and rubber production is down sharply. Gold and foreign exchange reserves have dipped from $222 million in 1960 to $158 million, and export earnings will drop this year from $70 million to $55 million. Nearly $2.5 billion in U.S. aid has only made South Viet Nam more dependent on—and more critical of—its friends.

Yet U.S. aid is essential not only to South Viet Nam's survival as a free nation; it is also helping subtly to foster what General Taylor called a "growing national character, a great national movement." The strategic hamlet program alone has given thousands of peasants their first experience of self-government: bolstered by U.S. economic aid, the experiment has also brought teachers, doctors and agricultural advisers to large areas that, in consequence, are undergoing what a top Vietnamese official calls "a social revolution, with a whole new scale of values."

As the Vietnamese clear and hold the countryside, Taylor said last week, "the emphasis will shift more to economic and social activities." In this realm alone, U.S. advisers admit, a vast amount remains to be done. Militarily, also, South Viet Nam still faces a long, hard fight. But the national effort is gathering momentum. Declared Maxwell Taylor: "South Viet Nam is moving toward victory because the South Vietnamese are fighting their own battle."

"Their Own Battle," *Time*, September 21, 1962.

Letter to America

Ho Chi Minh, the leader of Communist North Vietnam, often portrayed the war in Vietnam as a struggle of free people against an oppressive and unpopular South Vietnamese government backed by the United States. Minh held that the people of both North and South Vietnam were united in their efforts to create one independent nation, and that the United States was unjustly interfering in that praiseworthy goal. In this 1964 letter to the American magazine Minority of One, *Ho Chi Minh explains the righteousness of his cause to an American readership that, if told the truth, would logically not support their own government in challenging the cause of freedom and independence in Southeast Asia. Amidst his depiction of the injustices and crimes perpetrated against the Vietnamese people, Minh interjects phrases and ideas from the Declaration of Independence and the U.S. Constitution to equate the struggle in Vietnam with America's own fight for independence.*

I wish to convey to our American friends greetings of friendship together with this earnest appeal.

I hope that you will more clearly realize the bitter truth about South Vietnam which constitutes one half of our fatherland. An extremely atrocious war is raging there, a war which turns out to be the biggest, the most protracted, and the

North Vietnamese leader Ho Chi Minh hoped to unify north and south Vietnam.

bloodiest one now going on in the world. This so-called "special war" is actually a war of aggression waged by the U.S. Government and its agents, a war which is daily causing grief and suffering to our fourteen million compatriots in South Vietnam, and in which thousands of American youths have been killed or wounded. This "special war" is reducing to ashes our villages, destroying our fields, and devastating one half of our country; it has cost the American people thousands of millions of dollars. Furthermore, this war which is replete with horrible crimes, has not only infringed upon the freedom and independence of our compatriots in South Vietnam, but also besmeared the good reputation and good traditions of the American people.

The Vietnamese people are well aware that the American people want to live in peace and friendship with all other nations. I have been to the United States, and I understand that the Americans are a talented people strongly attached to justice.

The Vietnamese people never confuse the justice-loving American people and the U.S. Government which has committed numerous crimes against them in the past ten years. Those very saboteurs of our nation's independence and freedom are also the people who have betrayed the Declaration of Independence of the United States which highlights the truth that "all men are created equal," and the unalienable Rights of man, viz [specifically]. "Life, Liberty, and the pursuit of Happiness." . . .

For ten years now, U.S. Governments and their agents have tried to crush the resistance of a heroic people by the use of brutal force. They want to turn our fourteen million compatriots in South Vietnam into slaves, and the southern part of our country into a new-type colony and a military base with a view to menacing the independence of the Indochinese and other Southeast Asian countries and attacking North Vietnam. . . .

But facts have shown that the path of aggression followed by the U.S. imperialists in South Vietnam is only a dark "tunnel" as admitted by the late President John Kennedy.

The heroic people of South Vietnam are resolved not to balk at the guns of the aggressors and traitors. Our compatriots would rather sacrifice everything than live in slavery. So far, under the leadership of the National Front for Liberation, the patriotic forces in South Vietnam have daily grown in strength and enjoy an increasing prestige at home and abroad. More than half of the population and over two-thirds of the territory of South Vietnam have been liberated. . . .

From the bottom of their hearts, the Vietnamese people thank the workers', youth, students', and women's organizations, as well as progressive intellectuals, congressmen, and clergymen in the United States who have courageously raised their voices, staged demonstrations, exposed the criminal policy of aggression pursued by the U.S. government, and expressed their support for the just struggle of the patriotic forces in South Vietnam.

I wish to add the following for our American friends: Not only do we suffer because of the hardships and sacrifices imposed on our compatriots in South Vietnam, we also feel pity and sympathy for the American mothers and wives who have lost their sons or husbands in the unjust war carried out in South Vietnam by the U.S. militarists.

One cannot allow the U.S. Government and its agents to go on indefinitely perpetrating [carrying out] their dark designs. It is high time to stay [stop] their bloody hands. . . .

Demand that the U.S. Government let the Vietnamese people decide themselves their own internal affairs. The provisions of the 1954 Geneva Agreements on Vietnam recognizing the unalienable national rights of the Vietnamese people must be strictly respected. That is the only solution to the South Vietnam question which does not involve face-losing [embarrassment] for the United States.

I hope that this urgent appeal will reach the American people. Once again I wish to thank all American progressive intellectuals and people who, for the sake of justice and freedom, peace and the friendship between our two peoples, have valiantly opposed the U.S. Government's policy of aggression in South Vietnam.

I send you my best greetings.

Ho Chi Minh, Letter to the Editor, *Minority of One*, May 1964.

The Tonkin Gulf Resolution

In August 1964, two U.S. destroyers reported that they had been fired upon by North Vietnamese gunboats while staging operations in the Gulf of Tonkin. Although skeptics were unsure if these attacks ever occurred (the destroyer crews were also not sure themselves), the incident gave the United States the pretext to launch retaliatory strikes against North Vietnam. Previously, the United States had only played the role of advisor in helping the South fight the war within its own borders, but armed with this congressional resolution passed on August 7, President Lyndon Johnson ordered the bombing of North Vietnam. The Tonkin Gulf Resolution gave Johnson the power to pursue war for as long as he deemed necessary, and the president seized the opportunity to greatly expand America's role in the conflict.

To promote the maintenance of international peace and security in southeast Asia.

Whereas naval units of the Communist regime in Vietnam, in violation of the principles of the Charter of the United Nations and of international law, have deliberately and repeatedly attacked United States naval vessels lawfully present in international waters, and have thereby created a serious threat to international peace; and

Whereas these attacks are part of a deliberate and systematic campaign of aggression that the Communist regime in North Vietnam has been waging against its neighbors and the nations joined with them in the collective defense of their freedom; and

Whereas the United States is assisting the peoples of southeast Asia to protect their freedom and has no territorial, military or political ambitions in that area, but desires only that these peoples should be left in peace to work out their own destinies in their own way: Now, therefore, be it:

Resolved by the Senate and House of Representatives of the United States of America in Congress assembled, That the Congress approves and supports the determination of the President, as Commander in Chief, to take all necessary measures to repel any armed attack against the forces of the United States and to prevent further aggression.

Sec. 2. The United States regards as vi-

In response to attacks on U.S. destroyers, President Lyndon B. Johnson signs the Tonkin Gulf Resolution.

tal to its national interest and to world peace the maintenance of international peace and security in southeast Asia. Consonant [in agreement] with the Constitution of the United States and the Charter of the United Nations and in accordance with its obligations under the Southeast Asia Collective Defense Treaty, the United States is, therefore, prepared, as the President determines, to take all necessary steps, including the use of armed force, to assist any member or protocol state of the Southeast Asia Collective Defense Treaty requesting assistance in defense of its freedom.

Sec. 3. This resolution shall expire when the President shall determine that the peace and security of the area is reasonably assured by international conditions created by action of the United Nations or otherwise, except that it may be terminated earlier by concurrent resolution of the Congress.

Department of State Bulletin, August 29, 1964.

A Warning Against U.S. Escalation

As U.S. counsel to the French embassy in Vietnam, George W. Ball had witnessed the defeat of the modernized French army in the first Indochina War. He maintained his doubts that any force could overcome the will of the Viet Cong. When he became Lyndon Johnson's undersecretary of state, Ball consistently spoke out against the broadening of America's role in Vietnam. He rightly feared Johnson would

commit more and more troops to the region in the vain hope of besting a determined and battle-hardened Vietnamese peasant army. His July 1, 1965, memo to the president, "A Compromise Solution in South Vietnam," eloquently argued against the commitment of additional ground forces and urged that the United States cut its losses and get out of Vietnam. President Johnson admired Ball's resolution but ignored his advice.

(1) A Losing War: The South Vietnamese are losing the war to the Viet Cong. No one can assure you that we can beat the Viet Cong or even force them to the conference table on our terms, no matter how many hundred thousand white, foreign (U.S.) troops we deploy.

No one has demonstrated that a white ground force of whatever size can win a guerrilla war—which is at the same time a civil war between Asians—in jungle terrain in the midst of a population that refuses cooperation to the white forces (and the South Vietnamese) and thus provides a great intelligence advantage to the other side. Three recent incidents vividly illustrate this point: (a) the sneak attack on the Da Nang Air Base which involved penetration of a defense perimeter guarded by 9,000 Marines. This raid was possible only because of the cooperation of the local inhabitants; (b) the B52 raid that failed to hit the Viet Cong who had obviously been tipped off; (c) the search and destroy mission of the 173rd Air Borne Brigade which spent three days looking for the Viet Cong, suffered 23 casualties, and never made contact with the enemy who had obviously gotten advance word of their assignment.

(2) The Question to Decide: Should we limit our liabilities in South Vietnam and try to find a way out with minimal long-term costs?

The alternative—no matter what we may wish it to be—is almost certainly a protracted war involving an open-ended commitment of U.S. forces, mounting U.S. casualties, no assurance of a satisfactory solution, and a serious danger of escalation at the end of the road.

(3) Need for a Decision Now: So long as our forces are restricted to advising and assisting the South Vietnamese, the struggle will remain a civil war between Asian peoples. Once we deploy substantial numbers of troops in combat it will become a war between the U.S. and a large part of the population of South Vietnam, organized and directed from North Vietnam and backed by the resources of both Moscow and Peiping.

The decision you face now, therefore, is crucial. Once large numbers of U.S. troops are committed to direct combat, they will begin to take heavy casualties in a war they are ill-equipped to fight in a noncooperative if not downright hostile countryside.

Once we suffer large casualties, we will have started a well-nigh irreversible process. Our involvement will be so great that we cannot—without national humiliation—stop short of achieving our complete objectives. Of the two possibilities I think

humiliation would be more likely than the achievement of our objectives—even after we have paid terrible costs.

(4) Compromise Solution: Should we commit U.S. manpower and prestige to a terrain so unfavorable as to give a very large advantage to the enemy—or should we seek a compromise settlement which achieves less than our stated objectives and thus cut our losses while we still have the freedom of maneuver to do so.

(5) Costs of Compromise Solution: The answer involves a judgment as to the cost to the U.S. of such a compromise settlement in terms of our relations with the countries in the area of South Vietnam, the credibility of our commitments, and our prestige around the world. In my judgment, if we act before we commit substantial U.S. troops to combat in South Vietnam we can, by accepting some short-term costs, avoid what may well be a long-term catastrophe. I believe we tended grossly to exaggerate the costs involved in a compromise settlement. . . .

On balance, I believe we would more seriously undermine the effectiveness of our world leadership by continuing the war and deepening our involvement than by pursuing a carefully plotted course toward a compromise solution. In spite of the number of powers that have—in response to our pleading—given verbal support from feeling of loyalty and dependence, we cannot ignore the fact that the war is vastly unpopular and that our role in it is perceptibly eroding the respect and confidence with which other nations regard us. We have not persuaded either our friends or allies that our further involvement is essential to the defense of freedom in the cold war. Moreover, the [more] men we deploy in the jungles of South Vietnam, the more we contribute to a growing world anxiety and mistrust.

George Ball, Letter to Johnson, July 1, 1965.

Vietnam Is a Just Cause

Just after the Tonkin Gulf incident, President Johnson broadened America's role in Vietnam. In addition to a bombing campaign against the North, Johnson ordered the first American combat units into Vietnam in March 1965. These troops were soon given the task of conducting offensive action against Viet Cong and North Vietnamese regular forces. All of this was accomplished without the president ever asking Congress for a declaration of war against North Vietnam.

On the home front, Johnson's acts were met with growing protest at college campuses and elsewhere. Faced with this dissent—which was garnering media attention—Johnson had to rally support among the American people. In July 1965, Johnson made the decision

The first U.S. Marines deploy on the beaches of South Vietnam in March 1965.

to increase the number of U.S. troops in Vietnam. Knowing it would be an unpopular move, Johnson held a press conference in which he explained why the increase was necessary if the United States was to fulfill its pledge to save South Vietnam from Communist aggression.

My fellow Americans. Not long ago, I received a letter from a woman in the Midwest. She wrote:

> Dear Mr. President,
>
> In my humble way I am writing to you about the crisis in Vietnam. My husband served in World War II. Our country was at war. But now, this time, it's just something that I don't understand. Why?

Well, I've tried to answer that question dozens of times and more in practically every state in this Union. I have discussed it fully in Baltimore in April, in Washington in May, in San Francisco in June. And let me again now discuss it here in the East Room of the White House.

Why must young Americans, born into a land exultant and with hope and with golden promise, toil and suffer and sometimes die in such a remote and distant place?

The answer, like the war itself, is not an easy one. But it echoes clearly from the painful lessons of half a century.

Three times in my lifetime—in two world wars and in Korea—Americans have

gone to far lands to fight for freedom. We have learned at a terrible and a brutal cost that retreat does not bring safety, and weakness does not bring peace.

And it is this lesson that has brought us to Viet Nam.

This is a different kind of war. There are no marching armies or solemn declarations. Some citizens of South Viet Nam, at times with understandable grievances, have joined in the attack on their own Government.

But we must not let this mask the central fact that this is really war. It is guided by North Viet Nam and it is spurred by Communist China. Its goal is to conquer the south, to defeat American power and to extend the Asiatic dominion of communism.

And there are great stakes in the balance.

Most of the non-Communist nations of Asia cannot, by themselves and alone, resist the growing might and the grasping ambition of Asian communism.

Our power therefore is a very vital shield. If we are driven from the field in Viet Nam, then no nation can ever again have the same confidence in American promise or in American protection.

In each land, the forces of independence would be considerably weakened, and an Asia so threatened by Communist domination would certainly imperil the security of the United States itself.

We did not choose to be the guardians at the gate, but there is no one else. Nor would surrender in Viet Nam bring peace, because we learned from Hitler at Munich that success only feeds the appetite of aggression. The battle would be renewed in one country, and then another country bringing with it perhaps even larger and crueler conflict, as we have learned from the lessons of history.

Moreover, we are in Viet Nam to fulfill one of the most solemn pledges of the American nation. Three Presidents—President Eisenhower, President Kennedy and your present President—over eleven years have committed themselves and have promised to help defend this small and valiant nation.

Strengthened by that promise, the people of South Viet Nam have fought for many long years. Thousands of them have died. Thousands more have been crippled and scarred by war. And we just cannot now dishonor our word, or abandon our commitment, or leave those who believed us and who trusted us to the terror and repression and murder that would follow.

This, then, my fellow Americans, is why we are in Viet Nam.

Lyndon Johnson, Statement at a White House News Conference, July 28, 1965.

Chapter 2

In Country

In July 1965, President Lyndon B. Johnson and his administration decided to escalate the war in Vietnam. Fifty thousand combat troops were dispatched immediately to Vietnam to supplement to the 23,000 U.S. advisors already there. By year's end, over 184,000 U.S. military personnel would be in the country. The numbers continued to climb over the next few years. In December 1968 troop strengths reached their peak. Over half a million American soldiers were engaged in the fight over Vietnam.

In the early years, many U.S. combat troops came to Vietnam with faith in the government's anti-Communist crusade. They believed they were helping a democratic people to fend off aggression. What the Americans soon discovered, however, was that the government of South Vietnam was not very democratic and the people of South Vietnam were not very interested in another foreign military power trampling through their nation. The civilian popula-

tion was either apathetic or openly hostile, generating and sheltering the Viet Cong insurgents who fought a guerrilla war against the American invaders. Unable to tell friend from foe among the peasantry, the American soldiers became wary and suspicious of the people they were supposedly defending.

The hit-and-run tactics of the Viet Cong also unnerved and disoriented the American troops. The U.S. military had been accustomed to fighting set-piece battles in which enemy lines could be pushed back and land taken and held. In Vietnam, most battles were small skirmishes in jungle settings. Ambushes were common, as were booby traps and sniper fire. Flushing the enemy out proved problematic, since most were never seen in the dense undergrowth. Even if the Americans gained the upper hand in a firefight, their victories were bittersweet as the Viet Cong tended to disengage and melt back into the jungle when hard-pressed. Finally, when an area was secured, the U.S. troops never occupied it for long. They moved on, and eventually the secured areas were infested again by more Viet Cong who re-materialized from the surrounding countryside. Fighting an elusive enemy was frustrating and demoralizing, especially as comrades fell during engagements that had no territorial objectives and yielded no feeling that the enemy had been decisively defeated.

As the war progressed, the soldiers also got wind of the protests at home. Much of America's youth was taking to the streets in demonstrations against the government's war of aggression. News circulated of students burning draft cards and others using every measure to avoid induction. The soldiers—who were roughly the same age as the protestors back home—wondered why they had been sent to Vietnam while their peers could openly defy military service. Anger and jealousy ate at some soldiers; others, however, hoped the protest movement would grow and bring the war to an end. Regardless, the troops were saddled with the knowledge that they were fighting an unpopular war, and that had a devastating effect on morale.

Low morale and no clear-cut strategies for victory pushed some men in Vietnam to find ways of escaping the daily pressures. Drug abuse and alcoholism were rampant, and these often contributed to insubordination. Especially after President Nixon announced the first troop withdrawals from Vietnam in May 1969, no soldier wanted to take unnecessary risks knowing that he may soon be rotated home. There were instances in which soldiers openly defied orders to engage the enemy, and even cases in which soldiers murdered—or "fragged"—their more gung-ho officers. Most troops, however, became afflicted with "short-timer's syndrome"—merely doing the minimum asked of them while counting down the days they had left in their year-long tour of duty.

Of course, all of these disheartening aspects of military service in Vietnam do not account for the selflessness and bravery that many soldiers displayed. Often operating independently in small groups in an enemy-infested jungle, the troops bonded with each other, and that comradeship inspired acts of heroism. There are many accounts of loyalty that drove one man or a whole squad to brave enemy fire to rescue a wounded comrade. Although such acts are not uncommon to other wars, given the general malaise of the military and the pressures of fighting an unpopular war, the will to persevere in spite of this mental baggage seems unique. Thus to their credit, even with the knowledge that they might be fighting in vain, the soldiers in Vietnam fought on. And after the war was over, the combat troops shared a connection that was unlike any shared by veterans of other American wars.

Butchery Is Butchery

Philip Caputo served with the marines in Vietnam during 1965 and 1966. He entered the war believing that America would crush the Communist forces in short order. After serving only a few months of his duty counting U.S. and enemy casualties, Caputo's convictions changed. He saw the horrors of death and the mounting corpses while the U.S. soldiers seemed to make no headway against an elusive enemy. The wet weather and rugged terrain made him feel that even the land conspired against the Americans. In this excerpt from his famed memoir, A Rumor of War, *Caputo recounts how many soldiers in Vietnam*

U.S. Marines stand over a cowering Viet Cong prisoner of war.

shared his souring mood after a brief time in the country. He also reveals how the frustration and poor spirits of the soldiers contributed to and were a result of atrocities committed in the dehumanizing war.

The regiment's mood began to match the weather. We were a long way from the despair that afflicted American soldiers in the closing years of the war, but we had also traveled some emotional distance from the cheery confidence of eight months before. The mood was sardonic, fatalistic, and melancholy. I could hear it in our black jokes "Hey, Bill, you're going on patrol today. If you get your legs blown off can I have your boots?" I could hear it in the songs we sang. . . .

There was another side to the war, about which no songs were sung, no jokes made. The fighting had not only become more intense, but more vicious. Both we and the Viet Cong began to make a habit of atrocities. One of the 1st Batallion's radio operators was captured by an enemy patrol, tied up, beaten with clubs, then executed. His body was found floating in the Song Tuy Loan three days after his capture, with the ropes still around his hands and feet and a bullet hole in the back of his head. Four other marines from another regiment were captured and later discovered in a common grave, also tied up and with their skulls blasted open by an executioner's bullets. . . . A twenty-eight man patrol was ambushed by two hundred VC and almost annihilated.

Only two marines, both seriously wounded, lived through it. There might have been more survivors had the Viet Cong not made a systematic massacre of the wounded. After springing the ambush, they went down the line of fallen marines, pumping bullets into any body that showed signs of life. . . . The two men who survived did so by crawling under the bodies of their dead comrades and feigning death.

We paid the enemy back, sometimes with interest. It was common knowledge that quite a few captured VC never made it to prison camps; they were reported as "shot and killed while attempting to escape." Some line companies did not even bother taking prisoners; they simply killed every VC they saw, and a number of Vietnamese who were only suspects. The latter were usually counted as enemy dead, under the unwritten rule "If he's dead and he's Vietnamese, he's VC."

Everything rotted and corroded quickly over there: bodies, boot leather, canvas, metal, morals. Scorched by the sun, wracked by the wind and rain of the monsoon, fighting in alien swamps and jungles, our humanity rubbed off of us as the protective bluing rubbed off the barrels of our rifles. We were fighting in the cruelest kind of conflict, a people's war. It was no orderly campaign, as in Europe [during World War II], but a war for survival waged in a wilderness without rules or laws; a war in which each soldier fought for his own life and the lives of the men beside him, not caring who he killed in that personal cause or how many or in what manner and feeling only contempt for those who sought to impose on his savage struggle the mincing distinctions of civilized warfare—that code of battle-field ethics that attempted to humanize an essentially inhuman war. . . . Butchery was butchery, so who was to speak of rules and ethics in a war that had none?

Philip Caputo, *A Rumor of War.* New York: Henry Holt, 1977.

Another Bittersweet Victory

In the fall of 1967, the 173rd Airborne Brigade was one of many American units taking part in the Dak To campaign in the Central Highlands of South Vietnam. For four days the 173rd Airborne had been pinned down by enemy bunkers atop Hill 875, one of the many Viet Cong and North Vietnamese Army (NVA) strongholds in the region. On Thanksgiving Day, the American troops at the base were given orders to take the hill. Edward F. Murphy was one of those who made the charge up the slopes. In his memoir, Murphy recounts the exhilaration and determination the men felt as they rushed into action. But, as Murphy notes, the exaltation of reaching the top was quickly undercut when the Americans realized the hill had been mostly vacated and the elusive enemy had slipped

away again. Like so many firefights in Vietnam, the U.S. troops storming Hill 875 had been robbed of total victory and were faced with the wastefulness of their gallant charge by the number of casualties they had taken.

At 1100 Captain Leonard spoke into his radio. A preparatory barrage of 81mm mortar shells from the three companies' weapons crashed down in front of Bravo and Charlie [companies]. When the shelling ended Leonard looked at Lieutenant Lindseth and said, "Let's go."

Lindseth repeated the words to his platoon. Then he jumped up from his crouching position and ran uphill. Much to his surprise only desultory enemy fire greeted his charge. What are the gooks up to? he wondered.

Thirty meters from his jump-off spot Lindseth saw his first enemy bunker. Unhesitatingly, the young officer jumped right into the hole. Crumpled at its bottom lay a wounded North Vietnamese soldier. Lindseth poked him with his rifle barrel. The NVA was unconscious. Lindseth leapt from the bunker and continued his attack.

Around him other Bravo paratroopers raced across the torn ground. Screaming and yelling as loud as they could, they charged headlong toward the enemy.

"Geronimo!"

"Airborne!"

"Die, you f—ers!"

"All the way!"

Members of the 173 Airborne Brigade methodically make their way up Hill 875.

The epithets and obscenities rose to a crescendo, nearly drowning out the bursts of M16 and M60 fire from the paratroopers. . . .

By the time the lead paratroopers covered the first fifty meters, NVA mortar shells started dropping among them. Sharp blasts sent hot metal zinging across the hillside.

One round landed right behind [Captain] Connolly. He went to his knees, his ears ringing from the explosion. Blood ran from several shrapnel wounds. Ignoring them, Connolly arose. "Go! Go!" he yelled. Those paratroopers who'd sought cover came out and continued the charge. . . .

Dashing from cover to cover, crouching behind logs, firing his M16 in long, sweeping bursts, [Lieutenant] Proffitt closed in on Hill 875's summit. By the time he'd covered half the distance, Proffitt had begun to realize that only

31

intermittent enemy rifle fire and scattered mortar rounds hampered his progress. Could it be possible, he wondered, that the NVA were gone? Or were they simply holding their fire, drawing the paratroopers into an elaborate trap?

The same thoughts occurred to Colonel Johnson. From his chopper circling above the hill, Johnson could see the dark green-clad figures of his battalion rushing up the hillside. To his surprise, enemy resistance appeared minimal; only the occasional burst of an enemy mortar round seemed to be holding them back. . . .

Captain Leonard couldn't believe the good progress Bravo was making. At the beginning of the attack most of his Sky Soldiers had advanced cautiously, using classic fire and maneuver techniques. As they realized the enemy's resistance was practically nonexistent, they became bolder, running upright, yelling and screaming, "C'mon, you motherf—ers! Come out and fight," one youngster yelled as he darted past Leonard.

Concerned that his men were becoming careless, Leonard urged caution. "Toss grenades in those bunkers," he ordered. "There might be gooks hiding in there." . . .

At the forefront of the attack, Lieutenant Lindseth neared the summit. He was practically running now. He couldn't believe how close he was to the top. Ignoring the enemy mortars, he raced upward, jumped over a log, and was there—on top of Hill 875. In just twenty minutes Lindseth had completed an attack that had stalled two battalions for four days. Behind him other members of Bravo fanned out across the summit. Feeling relieved at his good fortune, but still fearful of a mortar attack, Lindseth found the deepest hole and jumped in. . . .

A few minutes later an enemy rifle round ripped into Captain Leonard's left leg, entering and exiting cleanly, spinning him around and down. Brushing away a medic's attempts to dress the wound—Leonard would not be denied this victory—he bounded up and limped on. Soon he joined Lindseth and the earlier arrivals at the top. Behind him others came, hooting and hollering in celebration of their success. . . .

The victory celebration was short-lived. In anticipation of an expected counterattack the three captains put their men into defensive positions. While they did so Johnson's helicopter landed. The colonel and Specialist 4th Class Jones hopped off. Johnson moved among the jubilant paratroopers, congratulating them on their success. Then the colonel moved down the hill to view the enemy positions. . . .

The main thing missing on the top of Hill 875 was enemy corpses. Only a few dozen were found in and around the top of the hill. Once again, the NVA had successfully eluded a decisive battle. Somehow, despite a near-constant pounding by artillery and aircraft, the NVA had managed to slip off Hill 875, taking their wounded and most of their dead with them. The paratroopers were denied the satisfaction of viewing the results of their victory.

Edward F. Murphy, *Dak To*. Novato, CA: Presidio Press, 1993.

Body Count

One of the most common U.S. military vehicles in Vietnam was the helicopter. Although helicopters were used in many roles in Vietnam, the attack helicopter used in close support with ground troops has become symbolic of America's strength and maneuverability in the war. Despite the image, the low-flying helicopter gunships were very vulnerable to enemy fire, and many crewmen did not survive their year-long tour of duty in Vietnam. Still, the helicopters were impressive weapons of war, and because of their ability to hover over a battlefield, they could cause substantial damage to enemy troops below. In this excerpt from a collection of personal narratives from the Ninth Air Cavalry Division, Ed Arthur, a door gunner (one who operated the machine gun on the open side door of a helicopter), relates his experiences of flying support during the advance of U.S. troops against the fortified positions of the North Vietnamese Army at Duc Pho in 1967. Arthur exhibits pure exhilaration as he catalogs the death and destruction he wreaks on the enemy.

We flew over APC [armored personnel carriers] with guys sitting all over them as though they were on a hayride or something. We checked out the terrain just ahead and flew back. I was hanging half out of the bird, motioning on the APCs. The young dudes waved at the bird, laughing and shouting, as though it was all a big game. We moved the APCs along carefully while trying to establish radio contact with somebody on the ground to tell those dudes to get off the tops of those vehicles. They were sitting ducks, horsing around, legs dangling over the sides, bouncing along.

I started to tell the skipper that they must have thought it was a goddamn picnic, but then spotted two NVA in a ditch, raising their weapons. I grabbed the only thing within quick reach, my M79 grenade launcher, which I never could fire worth a damn, swung it toward the gooks, and jerked the trigger, praying that the grenade would at least hit close enough to throw them off. The round exploded before I had time to think about what was happening. It landed right between the NVAs. Shrapnel sliced into the gut of one. The other was thrown up and out of the ditch.

"Go back over," I shouted. I wanted to make sure both gooks were out of action. . . .

Down close to the tree line was a guy standing against a tree to stay out of sight. I motioned the skipper to go over, then machine-gunned the gook right across his body with my M16. It was goddamn good to see him flop over. I dropped more Willie Peters [white phosphorus grenades] for the APCs, waving my arm to direct them, then saw another gook crouched in a ditch. I pumped most of a clip at him, blowing the top of his head right off. Next we were over several gooks crawling into a bunker that had bullets pouring out of it. I took a Willie Peter, pulled the pin, leaned far out of the bird, hanging by my left hand with my foot on the skid, and pitched the grenade into the bunker.

"Did you see how many went in there?"

"At least six."

They had to be dead, every last one of them. Smoke was pouring out of the bunker, and of course, there was no more firing from there. The skipper pulled away. I saw another gook running across an open space toward the beach. We were right up against the South China Sea. The gook was probably making for a village along the side of a hill at two o'clock. A Huey gunship followed him, M60 spitting up sand all around his feet. I waited for the NVA to fly apart. I knew what those M60 slugs could do. But the man kept running like mad, arms and legs going faster than I ever seen anyone run before.

I laughed and punched the radio button. "Hey, Skipper. Look'y there. Bet that guy is clocking better than anybody's ever done at the Olympics."

Hasselgrove looked at me, then back at the gook still running with all that machine-gun fire kicking up the sand under him, then back at me again, shaking his head. "Sick joke, Arthur."

I knew it, but pointed, laughing some more, saying to myself, Only don't think, Ed! Don't think, just laugh! "Goddamn if he's not making a world record. If I had my stopwatch. . . ."

That's when the whole side of the gook's face went, torn right off, but it wasn't the Huey that got him. He'd cleared the cloud of dust left by the M60, and the gunship had roared over him. I wondered how in the hell they had missed. What had got him was the .50-caliber machine gun from one of the APCs. Once again it was like it was in the movies when the film was slowed down. The guy was down in the dust and we were past him. I saw more NVAs cornered in a cane field and fired at them, figuring I probably got several. I was keeping a mental record of all my kills in this battle. After I ran out of ammo, in what little flying time was left, I dropped smoke grenades to help the APCs root out the remaining NVAs.

Mathew Brennan, *Headhunters: Stories from the First Squadron, Ninth Cavalry in Vietnam, 1965–1971.* Novato, CA: Presidio Press, 1987.

Booby Trap

Perhaps the American soldier's greatest fear in the jungles of Vietnam was falling victim to a Viet Cong (VC) booby trap. The VC were experts in producing a variety of deadly devices that ranged from spike traps to explosive mines. Unwary American troops tripped trigger wires that set off the booby traps. If the soldiers were not instantly killed by the device, they were often crippled for life.

Soldiers examine a shredded booby trap that narrowly missed them after a tripwire flung it from a tree.

Lewis B. Puller was a victim of a Viet Cong booby trap. Puller went to Vietnam in 1968, but was wounded just a few months after arriving when he stepped on a concealed explosive howitzer shell. In his autobiography, Fortunate Son, *Puller describes the tragic incident and the memories of the explosion that tore off his legs and damaged both of his hands.* Fortunate Son *won the Pulitzer Prize in 1992. Two years later, Puller committed suicide.*

A narrow trail led up the hill to the headquarters group, and as I approached, it never occurred to me that the thirty meters between my course and the commanders' position had not been secured. I knew only that the firepower advantage of the NVA [North Vietnamese Army] squad I had just encountered would be neutralized if I could reach the men milling at the crest of the hill. With only a few meters left to cover in my flight, a thunderous boom suddenly rent the air, and I was propelled upward with the acrid smell of cordite in my nostrils.

When I landed a few feet up the trail from the booby-trapped howitzer round that I had detonated, I felt as if I had been airborne forever. Colors and sound became muted, and although there was now a beehive of activity around me, all movement seemed to me to be in slow motion. I thought initially that the loss of my glasses in the explosion accounted for my blurred vision, and I had no idea that the pink mist that engulfed me had been caused by the vaporization of most of my right and left legs. As shock began to numb my body, I could see through a haze of pain that my right thumb and little finger were missing, as was most of my left hand, and I could smell the charred flesh, which extended from my right wrist upward to the elbow. I knew that I had finished serving my time in the hell of Vietnam.

As I drifted in and out of consciousness, I felt elated at the prospect of relinquishng my command and going home to my wife and unborn child. I did not understand why Watson, who was the first man to reach me, kept screaming, "Pray, Lieutenant, for God's sake, pray." I could not see the jagged shards of flesh and bone that had only moments before been my legs, and I did not realize until much later that I had been forever set apart from the rest of humanity.

For the next hour a frantic group of marines awaited the medevac [medical evacuation] chopper that was my only hope of deliverance and worked at keeping me alive. Doc Ellis knelt beside my broken body and with his thumbs kept my life from pouring out into the sand, until a tourniquet fashioned from a web belt was tied around my left stump and a towel was pressed tightly into the hole where my right thigh had joined my torso. My watch and rifle had been destroyed by the blast, and my flak jacket was in tatters; but I did manage to turn my undamaged maps and command of the platoon over to Corporal Turner during one of my lucid intervals. I also gave explicit orders to all the marines and corpsmen hovering around me that my wife was not to be told of my injuries until after the baby was born. There was, of course no possibility of compliance with my command, but the marines ministering to me assured me that my wishes would be honored. . . .

When the chopper finally arived, I was placed on a stretcher and gently carried to its entrance, where a helmeted crew chief and medevac surgeon helped me aboard. Someone had located my left boot which still contained its bloody foot and that, too, was placed on the stretcher with me.

As the chopper began its race toward the triage of the naval support hospital in Da Nang, I was only moments from death, but I remember thinking clearly before loosing consciousness that I was going to make it. I never again saw the third platoon of Golf Company, a re-markable group of young men with whom I had had the most intense male relationships of my life, and I felt guilty for years that I had abandoned them be-fore our work was finished.

Lewis B. Puller, *Fortunate Son*. Grove/Atlantic, 1991.

Platoon Medic

Every platoon in Vietnam had a crew of medics that went into the field with the fighting soldiers. A medic's job was to give aid to the wounded, usually during combat situations. Medics often risked their lives to help injured soldiers in the midst of a fire-fight. Such selfless bravery earned the "Docs," as the were referred to, the respect of the men they accompanied. Daniel E. Evans served as a combat platoon medic in the Thirty-Ninth Infantry. When he began his tour of duty in 1968, Evans was afraid that his training had not prepared him for the horrors of patching up soldiers while under enemy fire. Recalling his first combat experience in his autbiography, Evans notes how his desire to help his injured com-rades overcame his fears, and his medical expertise helped keep wounded men alive until evacuation helicopters arrived.

Total chaos. Carnage. It awed me. Sick-ened me. I was the medic trainee who couldn't watch the Vietnam casualty movies at Fort Sam. Giving a hypodermic injection, nauseated me. But this was no longer training or a movie. It was real, and I was stuck square in the middle of it.

Injured, wounded and dying men called for me.

"Doc, help me!"

"Medic!"

"Doc! You'd better take a look at Harvill's leg.". . .

Death. I had seen it neatly encased in body bags back at the morgue I helped build for the 9th Med. I had not seen it like this. . . .

They're gonna die, I thought. These men are gonna die if I can't help them.

"Medic!"

I switched into automatic mode, just like that, just like before. A part of me de-tached itself from the rest. The detached part of me shrugged its shoulders and watched me go to work as in the drills in casualty exercises back at Fort Sam.

Seid was still holding Harvill's head out of the water. I fished up his right leg. Ligaments and tendons dangled ragged from the raw hamburger mass of his thigh. The water was bright red around him. He was losing a lot of blood. Artery severed. I rippped the sleeve off my uni-form and used it as a tourniquet. Slapped field dressings onto his other wounds. All I could do right now. I moved on.

A geyser of water exploded a foot ahead of me.

Treatment on the fly. Everyone had some type of wound. I soon ran out of bandages. I ripped up my shirt and cut

off my trouser legs to use as tourniquets and bandages. I treated the men in the ditch, then crawled out onto the road to make house calls on those too sick to come to me.

Two medics courageously rush to evacuate an injured paratrooper from a battlefield in Vietnam.

I didn't mark the passing of time, but it suddenly came to me that the wounded men were no longer fighting. They were crawling out of the water like primordial salamanders. The rescue party's withering fire had driven off the ambushers. Only one sniper remained behind to cover his comrades withdrawl. He plinked at us to make us keep our heads down. . . .

I looked up and saw [medics Jim] Whitmore and [Ron] Miller ignoring the sniper, as I was. I had already lost my helmet and rifle and used up most of my uniform. Whitmore dropped down next to

Teddy Creech and flung open his medical aid bag. "A dust-off is on the way," he shouted to me.

Creech's left leg, still wearing its combat boot, lay discarded in the road next to the mauled Jeep. His other leg was twisted like that of a cloth puppet without joints. Blood and gray ooze gushed from his many wounds.

Whitmore started to move away. "This one's dead," he announced.

Creech's eyes slowly opened in the bloody mask that was his face. "I ain't dead yet," he croaked. "Give me a shot of morphine."

The bullet hole in Richard Forte's abdomen had sealed itself. His bloated belly told me all the bleeding was internal. There was little I could do for him. His face was the color of old ivory.

"It's alright. I'm okay, Doc," he groaned. "Doc, the others . . . they need you. Go help my buddies, Doc."

Where did the army get such men—thinking of others while they themselves were dying? . . .

When the medevac chopper arrived, it skimmed in low over the trees, dragged its tail, and sat down on the narrow road in an explosion of dust and sniper fire. Dust-off medics leaped out to assist with the evacuation while the crew chief knelt on the roadway with an M16 across his knees. . . .

Afterward, stunned and emotionally spent, I stood wearily in the middle of the road and stared without seeing the splotches and puddles of thick blood left around the smoldering Jeep. Patrols out sweeping the area had driven off the sniper. I was glad someone had thought to toss Creech's severed leg aboard the chopper. I don't think I could have checked my gorge otherwise.

"What happened to your clothes, soldier?" one of the batallion leaders demanded.

I wore only my boots and the remains of my jungle trousers. I had ripped off the legs for bandages and tourniquets.

"Where's your helmet and weapon, GI?"

I was too spent to answer. I stared at the blood on my hands. Red gloves. I fixated on them. I guessed I was qualified now to wear my Combat Medic Badge. A sinking hard knot feeling formed in the pit of my stomach. This is only the beginning, the feeling seemed to gloat. You ain't seen it all yet.

Daniel E. Evans and Charles W. Sasser, *Doc: Platoon Medic*. New York: Pocket Books, 1998.

Boosting Morale

Jeanne Christie was one of the many women who went to Vietnam to entertain battle-weary troops. Working with the American Red Cross's Supplemental Recreational Activity Overseas (SRAO) program, Christie and her colleagues ran recreation centers at base camps where soldiers could simply relax. She also was sent out by helicopter to entertain troops in the field. There she and her group talked to soldiers and played silly games with them to take their mind off the fighting. In this excerpt from Kathryn Marshall's book on women in Vietnam, Christie describes her routine as she visits a combat unit.

Basically, when we were out in the field the men loved anything we did. For instance, when we went into the LZs [Landing Zones] the guys would sit on the hill or whatever and watch us in total awe. Some of them would flock to you and talk as fast as they could; others couldn't say a thing. But all of them would stare. They knew every movement we made—nothing we did escaped them.

For those who couldn't talk with us, it must have seemed strange to have us drop in from the sky. For the others, it was a chance to laugh and get a bit of relief from the war. Most of the time we took audience-participation programs and Kool-Aid. The audience-participation programs were silly things: question and answer, flashcards, felt-tip pens, rubber bands. All of us had rubber bands, because they were a great ice-breaker. What we did was put a rubber band over a guy's pinky and thumb and tell them they had to get it off without using any part of their body. Eventually they'd start laughing and teasing each other, and before they knew it their minds were on something other than the war.

There were other crazy things we did to divert their attention from the war, but

the program was a simple one: the morale of the troops was what was most important. Unfortunately, we were also known as the—quote unquote—fun and games girls, which does not translate well back here in the States. When my children—many years later—asked me what I did in the war, the explanation I ended up with was that some people patched others up, some people shot others, but I played games.

So it was a specific program designed to help the morale of the military we supported. As silly as this may sound, we personified the American women to the men. We were their homes, their sisters, their mothers, their wives, their girlfriends. We were reminders of what they had lost and what they had to continue on for.

Kathryn Marshall, *In the Combat Zone: An Oral History of American Women in Vietnam, 1966–1975.* Boston: Little, Brown, 1987.

Helping the Helpless

Julie Forsythe grew up in a Quaker community in New Jersey. Quakers traditionally have opposed war on moral grounds, and during the Vietnam era, many became conscientious objectors and were released from military service because of their religion. Others, like Forsythe, volunteered to serve in Vietnam as civilian aid workers, helping injured Vietnamese peasants caught in the war. In 1972 Forsythe was stationed in Quang Ngai province where she gave relief to many civilians who had suffered burns and other wounds, mostly as a result of American bombing and artillery fire. In this recollection, Forsythe describes how she adapted to the horrors she encountered during her three-year stay in Vietnam. Forsythe remained dedicated to the people of Vietnam, and stayed behind after the United States pulled its troops out of the battered country.

I wasn't prepared for a lot of things I saw. Like the prison wards. Or once I was in surgery and they were doing amputations—this was right after I got to Quang Ngai—and I nearly passed out. Horrible. But the kids were the worst. Up to 40 percent of our patients were kids—we saw about a thousand people a year—because the kids are the ones who take the ducks out and take the water buffalo down to the river. And some yo-yo leaves a land-mine in the path and—pop! That's it. No, I wasn't prepared for how many kids were so badly damaged.

A lot of them came in with no arms and legs. And we saw kids with neck injuries from shrapnel, so that they were

President Johnson visits a hospital where American nurses care for Vietnamese peasants injured in the war.

entirely paralyzed. At times we took over the hospital's burn unit, where we saw the kids who'd been napalmed. Napalm is really grim stuff. What's so disgusting about it is that only oil stops the burning. Water doesn't stop the burning, so when kids get hit with napalm they run into the river and the stuff keeps burning—they keep burning. And listen, the most disgusting thing you've ever seen in your life is a child who's just totally burned. Right down to the muscle. It's very, very painful, and the treatment is brutally long. It's almost impossible to undo that kind of damage. Maybe under extremely sanitary conditions—which we didn't have—and with horrible, really horrible, scar tissue.

Other burns we saw were due to black marketeering. A lot of airplane fuel was ripped off from the Air Force and sold as cooking fuel. And when it's ignited—whoom! Really disgusting, those body burns.

We did the best we could for our patients, under tough conditions. There never seemed to be enough of us, though. The center had a Vietnamese staff of sixty. They included the prostheticists, the physical therapists, the people who made limbs, a maintenance department, a schoolteacher, a social worker, a nurse, and a physician's assistant. The Americans were my husband, Tom—he was the doctor—a physical therapist who was training the Vietnamese, a husband-and-wife team who were codirectors, and me. I did all the jobs that fell in the cracks.

My position was great, because I got to relate to everybody. I got to take patients back to their homes, for instance—which meant I was out in the countryside much of the time. . . .

I remember once Tom and I went up to the mountains to do an evaluation on a hill tribe. It was pretty desperate—they were pretty much living on leaves. Not long after we got to the village a woman came out of a hut and grabbed me "I want to show you a picture of my son," she said. "He was killed in the fighting." So I went inside. She showed me the picture, and then she started keening and weeping. And there was nothing I could do. Nothing but sit very quietly, listening to her. So that's what I did. I just sat and listened.

I don't know why that memory jumps out any more than the others. Because things like that were so much a part of what went on.

Kathryn Marshall, *In the Combat Zone: An Oral History of American Women in Vietnam, 1966–1975*. Boston: Little, Brown, 1987.

Combat Fatigue

In the dark, impenetrable jungles of Vietnam, American soldiers operated on a heightened sense of alert. They needed to be ready for possible ambush at all times. Even in villages and cities, the soldiers felt vulnerable because the enemy could be hiding among the civilian population. This constant hypersensitivity was physically and emotionally draining. Sleep was the only re-

*course. Although some new recruits in the field got very little sleep because of the fear that a snapped twig could signal an approaching Viet Cong, the veteran soldiers learned that one could not stay awake forever. As journalist Michael Herr discusses, combat troops often existed in a half-sleep, half-waking state that took its toll on performance and morale. In his book, Dis-*patches, *Herr equates this constant feeling of fatigue with the half-hearted American effort in fighting the war in Vietnam.*

Sometimes you'd get so tired that you'd forget where you were and sleep the way

An exhausted soldier dozes during a break from his watch.

you hadn't slept since you were a child. I know that a lot of people there never got up from that kind of sleep; some called them lucky (Never knew what hit him), some called them f——ed (If he'd been on the stick . . .), but that was worse than academic, everyone's death got talked about, it was a way of constantly touching and turning the odds, and real sleep was at a premium. (I met a ranger-recondo who could go to sleep just like that, say, "Guess I'll get some," close his eyes and be there, day or night, sitting or lying down, sleeping through some things but not others; a loud radio or a 105 firing outside the tent wouldn't wake him, but a rustle in the bushes fifty feet away would, or a stopped generator.) Mostly what you had was on the agitated side of half-sleep, you thought you were sleeping but you were really just waiting. Night sweats, harsh functionings of consciousness, drifting in and out of your head, pinned to a canvas cot somewhere, looking up at a strange ceiling or out through a tent flap at the glimmering night sky of a combat zone. Or dozing and waking under mosquito netting in a mess of slick sweat, gagging for air that wasn't 99 percent moisture, one clean breath to dry-sluice your anxiety and the backwater smell of your own body. But all you got and all there was were misty clots of air that corroded your appetite and burned your eyes and made your cigarettes taste like swollen insects rolled up and smoked alive, crackling and wet.

There were spots in the jungle where you had to have a cigarette going all the time, whether you smoked or not, just to keep the mosquitoes from swarming into your mouth. War under water, swamp fever and instant involuntary weight control, malarias that could burn you out and cave you in, put you into twenty-three hours of sleep a day without giving you a minute of rest, leaving you there to listen to the trance music that they said came in with terminal brain funk. ("Take your pills, baby," a medic in Can Tho told me. "Big orange ones every week, little white ones every day, and don't miss a day whatever you do. They got strains over here that could waste a heavyset fella like you in a week.") Sometimes you couldn't live with the terms any longer and headed for air-conditioners in Danang and Saigon. And sometimes the only reason you didn't panic was that you didn't have the energy.

Every day people were dying there because of some small detail that they couldn't be bothered to observe. Imagine being too tired to snap a flak jacket closed, too tired to clean your rifle, too tired to guard a light, too tired to deal with the half-inch margins of safety that moving through the war often demanded, just too tired to give a f—— and then dying behind that exhaustion. There were times when the whole war itself seemed tapped of its vitality: epic enervation, the machine running half-assed and depressed, fueled on the watery residue of last year's war-making energy. Entire divisions would function in a bad dream state, acting out a weird set of moves without any connection to their source. Once I talked for maybe five minutes with a sergeant who had just brought his squad in from a long patrol before I realized that the dopey-dummy film over his eyes and the fly abstraction of his words were coming from deep sleep. He was standing there at the bar of the NCO club with his eyes open and a beer in his hand, responding to some dream conversation far inside his head. It really gave me the creeps—this was the second day of the Tet Offensive, our installation was more or less surrounded, the only secure road out of there was littered with dead Vietnamese, information was scarce and I was pretty touchy and tired myself—and for a second I imagined that I was talking to a dead man. When I told him about it later he just laughed and said, "S——, that's nothing. I do that all the time."

Michael Herr, *Dispatches*. Alfred A, Knopf, 1977.

Chapter 3

War at Home

While U.S. soldiers fought in the jungles of Vietnam, another war erupted in the streets of America. A steadily growing legion of demonstrators stood up to government foreign policy makers in an attempt to end American military involvement in Southeast Asia. The protesters were mostly young; often the same age as the men serving the nation in Vietnam. They had adopted some of the counterculture beliefs of the 1950s and many had begun to examine the price of conformity and unquestioning faith in authority. They married these ideals to the belief in taking action, hoping that the huge number of baby boom children could find a voice loud enough to change a national agenda. The adherents ranged from radicals to idle peaceniks, but the antiwar platform helped galvanize them and gave shape to a more politically conscious generation.

Although homegrown opposition to American wars was not unique to the Vietnam era, the degree to which protest of the war in Vietnam influenced politics from the White House to the grassroots level was unprecedented. The antiwar movement, however, did not start out with such lofty aims. In 1965, when Lyndon Johnson chose to escalate the war, antiwar sentiment took root in universities. It was by no means a movement yet, but rather a collection of academics (mainly professors and students of political theory) taking issue with American foreign policy. To offer their opinions for debate, university faculty staged "teach-ins" with students at campuses such as Harvard and Berkeley. The "teach-ins" grew in popularity and were soon emerging at other colleges across the nation.

The universities were the hotbed of radical thought. New campus organizations sprang up based on an antiwar platform, while established organizations incorporated opposition to the war into their agendas. Radicals from Students for a Democratic Society (which had been around since 1960) took the cause one step further, organizing the first antiwar demonstration in Washington, D.C., in April 1965. The event drew a crowd of 15,000, but this was only a hint of what was to come. As U.S. involvement expanded and larger numbers of casualty reports reached American television, the protest movement took off. By 1967, a massive antiwar demonstration in Washington attracted more than 100,000 participants.

By this time, the movement had grown beyond university campuses. Now political leaders joined students and theorists to take a stand against the American government. Some of these politicians were sincere in their peace platforms, others certainly understood the power of potential voters. The Civil Rights movement also united with the antiwar demonstrators around 1967. Members of the Student Nonviolent Coordinating Committee, for example, argued that a high percentage of combat soldiers in Vietnam were black and that America was perpetrating this war both to squash the freedom of oppressed people oversees and to rid itself of unwanted ghetto youth. Although their aims sometimes conflicted, the war protesters and Civil Rights activists furthered each others' causes by bringing these issues to the national spotlight.

Complacent America's response to the antiwar movement was not enthusiastic. While some may have been swayed by protesters' arguments and conviction, others were decidedly repulsed by scruffy youths clashing with police. In fact throughout the early years of the war, public support for American policy never wavered significantly. The tide began to turn, however, in 1968. In that year, the North Vietnamese Tet Offensive showed how vulnerable American troops were in Vietnam and just how far the military was from securing the nation. Respected newsmen like Walter Cronkite resignedly acknowledged that the government seemed to be no closer to winning the war than when it started. Coupled with this disheartening fact was the news of protests at the Democratic National Convention in Chicago. In August, thousands of demonstrators descended on the convention to protest the Democratic Party's choice of candidates. The demonstrators were met by the city's unrestrained police force and local national guardsmen. Violence erupted at night, and many protesters were beaten and gassed in what bystanders later described as a police riot. Middle-America was shocked at the disturbing images of the nation's bleeding youth at home and abroad.

The Chicago riots, however, disrupted the movement's momentum, and an announcement in 1969 by then president Richard Nixon took even more wind out of its sails. Nixon stated he would begin bringing troops home from Vietnam immediately. The public at large believed this signaled that an end to the war was in sight. Nixon had not bowed to pressure since he vowed to "win the peace" in Vietnam, but he had successfully undermined the antiwar movement. Demonstrations, however, continued for as long as U.S. personnel remained in Vietnam. Nixon even re-energized the movement in 1970 when he ordered U.S. troops into Cambodia. Still by that time, the war was drawing to a close and the voices of protest were often considered too strident for the outcome of the conflict. Regardless, the movement had ultimately achieved its goal. And it left a lasting legacy—a generation that would continually question government and all forms of authority, and one that would face tough social issues in hopes of fostering a better society.

Students Organize Against the War

Lyndon Johnson's decision to escalate U.S. involvement in Vietnam sparked the first coordinated protests of the war. The initial protesters came from the faculty and students of prestigious colleges such as Harvard and Berkeley. Early protest took the form of spreading information about wrongheaded government policies. It was not until more college campuses joined in the struggle that more radical actions were taken. The May 2nd Movement (M2M) was one of the earliest resistance movements that promoted direct action. Named after the date of the first large Vietnam protest rallies in the United States, M2M was a student organization that encouraged young men to burn their draft cards in defiance of the government. It also visited industries in the hope of persuading workers to strike against the production of munitions and other wartime supplies. In M2M's 1965 manifesto, the group lays out its grievances and its commitment to action.

We, as students in the richest but most brutally confused country in the world, cannot understand that world and our part in it with the a-historical education we receive in our universities. In order to make ourselves into effective social beings and in order to discover, sharpen, and use the power of our knowledge, we should organize ourselves in the broadest possible way to combat that lack of education. For it is a lack, a vacuum, that leads to political degeneration and default. The May 2nd Movement was formed to fight against a politics of default, specifically by organizing student protest and revolt against our government's savage war on the people of Vietnam. . . .

The major issue facing U.S. students at this time is the war against the people of Vietnam. This war is also against the interests of the students and almost the entire population of the United States. Nine billion dollars has already been cut from

Student protesters hold placards that read "If your conscience demands it, refuse to serve in the armed forces."

the ever-decreasing "peace" portion of the federal budget. The war has been used against steel workers, who were told that they were not permitted to strike because of the "national emergency." The administration will demand that black Americans stop protesting in an attempt to cover angry faces with a mask of "national unity."

Most people realize that the U.S. is not fighting for freedom and democracy in Vietnam, that the Vietnamese people want nothing more than the U.S. to get out. We say to those who are being forced to kill and die for the interests of imperialism—don't go. The May 2nd Movement is launching an anti-induction campaign on the campuses. This campaign will organize existing resistance to the draft, based on the refusal to fight against the people of Vietnam. Each campus and each community should say, "No one from this college (or community) should be drafted." Declarations and literature will be circulated, forums and meetings held, demonstrations organized and acts of disobedience engaged in. The theme will be, "We Won't Go."

We are beginning a program of approaching workers at the factory gate to talk to them about the war in Vietnam and why it is against the interests of workers. This project comes out of the understanding that while students make up an important section of the population, industrial workers make, load and transport the goods, and are therefore the key for stopping the war in Vietnam—for stopping the whole system. While workers' militancy has become more apparent in recent years, we realize that organizing a radical workers' movement in this country is a long range goal, and one that essentially must be done by workers. All the more reason to begin projects now to involve workers in the peace movement and as allies of the student.

Some chapters of May 2 plan campaigns to donate blood and other medical aid to the National Liberation Front of South Vietnam, to concretely show our support for national liberation struggles. Receiving blood from U.S. college students will be a terrific morale boost to the Vietnamese people. Collecting pledges for blood on campus can also show where the administration stands, as collecting for civil rights did at Berkeley. . . .

May 2nd chapters put forward the idea that students must fight for control of their schools, and that by working together we can win fundamental changes in our day-to-day life. . . .

[M2M sponsored] study groups, such as on Vietnam, are meant for learning what is vital but not taught within the school. They are unlike most classes, where alleged experts provide descriptions of things for us to feed back in tests. The members of a study group come together to help each other increase their understanding of areas they feel necessary in order to be better able to fight for social change. The study group develops an analysis of events which is not right or wrong because a professor says so, but is judged by whether it aids in projecting the strategy and tactics of political struggle.

Our ideas have to correspond to reality if we are to organize large numbers of people to fight against a brutal system. We are in the process of developing an ideology based on anti-imperialism and support for the struggles of national liberation. To have an ideology means that we have beliefs based on studied understanding and analysis of the world situation. We put those beliefs forward for debate and for testing and if they are proven, we base our actions upon them. Our ideology enables us to see through events that confuse and mislead. Many people who are against the war in Vietnam, but who are "non-ideological," are deceived by Johnson's peace offensive. They believe, because it would be nice if it were true, that the administration's calls for negotiations represent a real desire to end the war. . . .

M2M is building an organization of students that recognizes, and works to satisfy, our needs as students and as men and women. These needs are inseparable from the worldwide struggle for liberation. One can choose to oppose this struggle, or to join it. To oppose it is to be a murderer. To join together and fight to change this murderous society is the only way for any of us to live with decency and dignity. We will succeed when large numbers of students have the insight, the dedication and the will to organize themselves, to join the struggle with their sections of the population, and to see it through.

Excerpt of Manifesto of May 2nd Movement, 1965.

America's War on the Impoverished and Oppressed

Between 1966 and 1968, over 40 percent of U.S. combat troops fighting in Vietnam were black. Most were assigned to frontline units and casualties among black soldiers ran high. Civil Rights leaders in the *United States were quick to point out that it seemed the American government was willing to sacrifice black youth while many white males were hiding out on college campuses and avoiding the draft.*

The Reverend Martin Luther King Jr. began speaking out against this discrimination and the war in general in 1966. In April 1967, King led an antiwar march in Chicago that attracted over five thousand people. That same month, he delivered his historic Beyond Vietnam speech. Gathered at a church in New York, a crowd listened as King argued that the government was fighting a war in Southeast Asia when it should be fighting a war against poverty at home. To King, it was the poor and oppressed who were suffering the most from the callous war. Both the peasants of Vietnam and the dispossessed blacks of American ghettos were being denied the ideals of liberty and equality on which the United States was founded.

Since I am a preacher by trade, I suppose it is not surprising that I have seven major reasons for bringing Vietnam into the field of my moral vision. There is at the outset a very obvious and almost facile connection between the war in Vietnam and the struggle I, and others, have been waging in America. A few years ago there was a shining moment in that struggle. It seemed as if there was a real promise of hope for the poor—both black and white—through the Poverty Program.

The Reverend Martin Luther King Jr. spoke forcefully against the Vietnam War.

Perhaps the more tragic recognition of reality took place when it became clear to me that the war was doing far more than devastating the hopes of the poor at home. It was sending their sons and their brothers and their husbands to fight and to die in extraordinarily high proportions relative to the rest of the population. We were taking the young black men who had been crippled by our society and sending them 8000 miles away to guarantee liberties in Southeast Asia which they had not found in Southwest Georgia and East Harlem. So we have been repeatedly faced with the cruel irony of watching Negro and white boys on TV screens as they kill and die together for a nation that has been unable to seat them together in the same schools. So we watch them in brutal solidarity burning the huts of a poor village, but we realize that they would never live on the same block in Detroit. I could not be silent in the face of such cruel manipulation of the poor.

Then came the build-up in Vietnam, and I watched the program [become] broken and eviscerated as if it were some idle political plaything of a society gone mad on war, and I knew that America would never invest the necessary funds or energies in rehabilitation of its poor so long as Vietnam continued to draw men and skills and money like some demonic, destructive suction tube. So I was increasingly compelled to see the war as an enemy of the poor and to attack it as such.

My third reason grows out of my experience in the ghettos of the North over the last three years—especially the last three summers. As I have walked among the desperate, rejected and angry young men, I have told them that Molotov cocktails and rifles would not solve their problems. I have tried to offer them my deepest compassion while maintaining my conviction that social change comes most meaningfully through non-violent action. But, they asked, what about Vietnam? They asked if our own nation wasn't using massive doses of violence to solve its problems, to bring about the changes it wanted. Their questions hit home, and I knew that I could never again raise my voice against the violence of the oppressed in the ghettos without having first spoken clearly to the greatest purveyor of violence in the world today—my own government. . . .

And as I ponder the madness of Vietnam, my mind goes constantly to the people of that peninsula. I speak now not of the soldiers of each side, not of the junta in Saigon, but simply of the people who have been living under the curse of war for almost three continuous decades. I think of them, too, because it is clear to me that there will be no meaningful solution there until some attempt is made to know them and their broken cries. . . .

They languish under our bombs and consider us—not their fellow Vietnamese—the real enemy. They move sadly and apathetically as we herd them off the land of their fathers into concentration camps where minimal social needs are rarely met. They know they must move or be destroyed by our bombs. So they go. . . .

What do the peasants think as we ally ourselves with the landlords and as we refuse to put any action into our many words concerning land reform? What do they think as we test out our latest weapons on them, just as the Germans tested our new medicine and new tortures in the concentration camps of Europe? Where are the roots of the independent Vietnam we claim to be building? . . .

Now there is little left to build on—save bitterness. Soon the only solid physical foundations remaining will be found at our military bases and in the concrete of the concentration camps we call "fortified hamlets." The peasants may well wonder if we plan to build our new Vietnam on such grounds as these. Could we blame them for such thoughts? We must speak for them and raise the questions they cannot raise. These too are our brothers. . . .

At this point, I should make it clear that while I have tried here to give a voice to the voiceless of Vietnam . . . , I am as deeply concerned about our own troops there as anything else. For it occurs to me that what we are submitting them to in Vietnam is not simply the brutalizing process that goes on in any war where armies face each other and seek to destroy. We are adding cynicism to the process of death, for our troops must know after a short period there that none of the things we claim to be fighting for are really involved. Before long they must know that their government has sent them into a struggle among Vietnamese, and the more sophisticated surely realize that we are on the side of the wealthy and the secure while we create a hell for the poor.

Somehow this madness must cease. I speak as a child of God and brother to the suffering poor of Vietnam and the poor of America who are paying the double price of smashed hopes at home and death and corruption in Vietnam. I speak as a citizen of the world, for the world as it stands aghast at the path we have taken. I speak as an American to the leaders of my own nation. The great initiative in this war is ours. The initiative to stop must be ours.

Martin Luther King Jr., "Beyond Vietnam" Speech, April 4, 1967.

A Challenge to the Current Administration

By 1967, antiwar activists in the Democratic Party were distraught that no politician had risen to challenge Lyndon Johnson's conduct during the war in Vietnam. In that year, several of these Democrats convinced Minnesota senator Eugene McCarthy to run against Johnson for the Democratic ticket in the coming election. No one expected that Johnson—who had a strong popularity rating—would be defeated, but the antiwar supporters hoped that McCarthy's bid would at least force a discussion of American policies in Vietnam. McCarthy, however, canvassed college campuses for support and soon had a huge army of America's youth behind him. In his nomination speech, McCarthy argued that America was paying a high price for its war in Vietnam. The current Democratic administration was willing to spend billions of dollars and waste tens of thousands of America's young men without any end in sight. McCarthy insisted a change was needed.

Since I first said that I thought the issue of Vietnam and the issues related to it should be raised in the primaries of the country I have talked with Democratic leaders from about 25 to 26 states. I've talked particularly to candidates for re-election to the Senate—Democratic candidates—some House members and also to students on campus and to other people throughout the country.

My decision to challenge the President's position and the Administration['s] position has been strengthened by recent announcements out of the Administration, the evident intention to escalate and to intensify the war in Vietnam, and . . . the absence of any positive indication or suggestion for a compromise or for a negotiated political settlement.

I am concerned that the Administration seems to have set no limit to the price which it's willing to pay for a military victory. Let me summarize the cost of the war up to this point:

The physical destruction of much of a small and weak nation by military operations of the most powerful nation in the world.

One hundred thousand to 150,000 civilian casualties in South Vietnam alone, to say nothing of the destruction of life and property in North Vietnam.

The uprooting and the fracturing of the structure of the society of South Vietnam where one-fourth to one-third of the population are now reported to be refugees.

For the United States as of yesterday over 15,000 combat dead and nearly 95,000 wounded through November.

A monthly expenditure in pursuit of the war amounting somewhere between $2-billion and $3-billion.

I am also concerned about the bearing of the war on other areas of the United States responsibility, both at home and abroad.

The failure to appropriate adequate funds for the poverty program here, for housing, for education and to meet other national needs and the prospect of additional cuts as a condition to the possible passage of the surtax tax bill.

The drastic reduction of our foreign aid program in other parts of the world.

A dangerous rise in inflation and one of the indirect and serious consequences of our involvement in Vietnam, the devaluation of the British pound, which in many respects is more important east of Suez today than the British Navy.

In addition, there is growing evidence of a deepening moral crisis in America—discontent and frustration and a disposition to take extralegal if not illegal actions to manifest protest.

I am hopeful that this challenge which I am making, which I hope will be supported by other members of the Senate and other politicians, may alleviate at least in some degree this sense of political helplessness and restore to many people a belief in the processes of American politics and of American government. . . .

To say that I'm—as I'm sure I shall be charged—I am not for peace at any price, but for an honorable, rational and political solution to this war, a solution which I believe will enhance our world position, encourage the respect of our allies and our potential adversaries, which will permit us to give the necessary attention to other commitments both at home and abroad, military and non-military and leave us with resources and moral energy to deal effectively with the pressing domestic problems of the United States itself.

In this—this total effort—I believe we can restore to this nation a clearer sense of purpose and of dedication to the achievement of our traditional purposes as a great nation in the 20th century.

Eugene McCarthy, Declarations of Candidacy for the Democratic Nomination for President, 1967.

Musical Protest

When protest of the Vietnam War took to the streets, it was accompanied by music. Singers and songwriters turned the feelings of the day into folk, rock, and soul ballads that pervaded college campuses and were quickly picked up by radio. The music gave protesters—especially young people—a rallying cry. And once the sentiments hit the airwaves, protest songs spread the antiwar message from coast to coast. Country singer Joe McDonald was virtually an unknown performer when he appeared at the Woodstock music festival in New York in 1969. With his folk band, Country Joe and the Fish, McDonald captured the mood of the young crowd and the antiwar movement when his band played the satirical "I-Feel-Like-I'm-Fixin'-to-Die Rag." The one performance catapulted Country Joe and the Fish into the spotlight, and the song became a protest anthem for years to come.

I-Feel-Like-I'm-Fixin'-to-Die Rag

Yeah, come on all of you, big strong men
Uncle Sam needs your help again.
He's got himself in a terrible jam
Way down yonder in Vietnam
So put down your books and pick up a gun,
We're gonna have a whole lotta fun.

And it's one, two, three,
What are we fighting for?
Don't ask me, I don't give a damn,
Next stop is Vietnam;
And it's five, six, seven,
Open up the pearly gates,
Well there ain't no time to wonder why,
Whoopee! we're all gonna die.

Well, come on generals, let's move fast;
Your big chance has come at last.
Gotta go out and get those reds —
The only good commie is the one who's dead
And you know that peace can only be won
When we've blown 'em all to kingdom come.

And it's one, two, three,
What are we fighting for?
Don't ask me, I don't give a damn,
Next stop is Vietnam;
And it's five, six, seven,
Open up the pearly gates,
Well there ain't no time to wonder why
Whoopee! we're all gonna die.

Huh!

Well, come on Wall Street, don't move slow,
Why man, this is war au-go-go.
There's plenty good money to be made
By supplying the Army with the tools of the trade,
Just hope and pray that if they drop the bomb,
They drop it on the Viet Cong.

Country Joe McDonald inspired the crowd at Woodstock with his antiwar song.

And it's one, two, three,
What are we fighting for?
Don't ask me, I don't give a damn,
Next stop is Vietnam.
And it's five, six, seven,
Open up the pearly gates,
Well there ain't no time to wonder why
Whoopee! we're all gonna die.

Well, come on mothers throughout the
    land,

Pack your boys off to Vietnam.
Come on fathers, don't hesitate,
Send 'em off before it's too late.
Be the first one on your block
To have your boy come home in
    a box.

And it's one, two, three,
What are we fighting for?
Don't ask me, I don't give a damn,
Next stop is Vietnam.
And it's five, six, seven,
Open up the pearly gates,
Well there ain't no time to wonder why,
Whoopee! we're all gonna die.

Country Joe and the Fish, "I-Feel-Like-I'm-Fixin'-to-Die Rag."
Reprinted by permission of Fantasy Recording Studios.

Thoughts on Induction

In one of his many memoirs of his life during the Vietnam era, author Tim O'Brien recalls his thoughts and feelings in the weeks just after he received his draft notice in 1968. Like many other young people at the time, O'Brien had been deferring military service because he was enrolled in college. In 1968, however, O'Brien graduated and within a short time his induction papers arrived. Since college campuses were rife with student protests of the war, O'Brien was not oblivious to the rationale of avoiding the draft, but he was also torn by the expectations of his family and community to serve his country. With the summer fading fast, O'Brien had to decide what stance he would take in regard to military service in Vietnam.

The summer of 1968, the summer I turned into a soldier, was a good time for talking about war and peace. . . . So with friends and acquaintances and townspeo-ple, I spent the summer in Fred's antiseptic cafe, drinking coffee and mapping out arguments on Fred's napkins. . . .

College friends came to visit: "Too bad. I hear you're drafted. What will you do?"

I said I didn't know, that I'd let time decide. Maybe something would change, maybe the war would end. Then we'd turn to discuss the matter, talking long, trying out the questions, sleeping late in the mornings. . . .

I was persuaded then, and I remain persuaded now, that the war was wrong. And since it was wrong and since people were dying as a result of it, it was evil. Doubts, of course, hedged all this: I had neither the expertise nor the wisdom to synthesize answers; the facts were clouded; there was no certainty as to the kind of government that would follow a North Vietnamese victory or, for that matter, an American victory, and the specifics of the conflict were hidden away—partly in men's minds, partly in the archives of government, and partly in buried, irretrievable history. The war, I thought, was wrongly conceived and poorly justified. But perhaps I was mistaken, and who really knew, anyway?

Piled on top of this was the town, my family, my teachers, a whole history of the prairie. Like magnets, these things pulled in one direction or the other, almost physical forces weighting the problem, so that, in the end, it was less reason and more gravity that was the final influence. . . .

In the basement of my house I found some scraps of cardboard. I printed obscene words on them. I declared my intention to have no part of Vietnam. With delightful viciousness, a secret will, I declared the war evil, the draft board evil, the town evil in its lethargic acceptance of it all. For many minutes, making up the signs, making up my mind, I was outside the town. I was outside the law. . . .

On the cardboard, my strokes of bright red were big and ferocious looking. The language was clear and certain and burned with a hard, defiant, criminal, blasphemous sound. I tried reading it aloud. I was scared. I was sad.

Later in the evening I tore the signs into pieces and put the shreds in the garbage can outside. . . .

I'd never been a demonstrator, except in the loose sense. True, I'd taken a stand in the school newspaper on the war, trying to show why it seemed wrong. But, mostly, I'd just listen.

"No war is worth losing your life for," a college acquaintance used to argue. "The issue isn't a moral one. It's a matter of efficiency: What's the most efficient way to stay alive when your nation is at war? That's the issue."

But others argued that no war is worth losing your country for, and when asked about the case when a country fights a wrong war, those people just shrugged.

Most of my college friends found easy paths away from the problem, all to their credit. Deferments for this and that. Letters from doctors or chaplains. It was hard to find people who had to think much about the problem.

On August 13, I went to the bus depot. A Worthington [Minnesota] *Daily Globe* photographer took my picture standing by a rail fence with four other draftees. . . .

At noon the next day our hands were in the air. . . . We recited the oath—some of us loudly and daringly, others in bewilderment. It was a brightly lighted room, wood paneled. A flag gave the place the right colors. There was smoke in the air. We said the words, and we were soldiers.

I'd never been much of a fighter. I was afraid of bullies: frustrated anger. Still, I deferred to no one. Positively lorded myself over inferiors. And on top of that was the matter of conscience and conviction, uncertain and surface-deep but pure nonetheless. I was a confirmed liberal. Not a pacifist, but I would have cast my ballot to end the Vietnam war, I would have voted for Eugene McCarthy, hoping he would make peace. I was not soldier material, that was certain.

But I submitted. All the soul searchings and midnight conversations and books and beliefs were voided by abstention, extinguished by forfeiture, for lack of oxygen, by a sort of sleepwalking default. It was no decision, no chain of ideas or reasons, that steered me into the war.

A war protester burns his draft card in a public display of antiwar sentiment.

It was an intellectual and physical stand-off, and I did not have the energy to see it to an end. I did not want to be a soldier, not even an observer to war. But neither did I want to upset a peculiar balance between the order I knew, the people I knew, and my own private world. It was not just that I valued that order. I also feared its opposite—inevitable chaos, censure, embarrassment, the end of everything that had happened in my life, the end of it all.

Tim O'Brien, *If I die in a Combat Zone: Box Me Up and Ship Me Home.* New York: Dell, 1973.

Dodging the Draft

Almost 27 million men were of draft age during the Vietnam War. Of those men between the ages of eighteen and a half and twenty-six, 16 million never served. Many were disqualified for medical reasons or religious convictions. Others had their induction legally deferred while they were attending school. Some, not all, used these exemptions to purposefully dodge the draft.

About 570,000 young men became draft dodgers to avoid service in Vietnam. While some of these claimed legal exemptions, others were openly defiant. Resisters spoke out against the war and often burned their draft cards in protest. Their defiance, however, had consequences. Draft evasion was a crime, and draft resisters were subject to arrest and imprisonment. This impelled a large number of draft dodgers to flee the country, typically crossing the border into Canada or Mexico. Ron Stone was a draft dodger who fled to Canada in 1969 just prior to receiving his induction papers. Stone lived in Canada for seven years where he was continually hounded by the FBI and the draft board. When the federal case against him was dropped in 1975, Stone returned to the United States. He recounted his experiences for a book on resisting the draft.

I let it be known to everyone that there was absolutely no way I was going to serve in Nixon's army, and there was absolutely no way I was going to serve in Vietnam. I did everything I had to do as a college student to stay out of the draft—I kept my course load up, I kept my grades up, I took the tests that you had to take. But, even having worked as hard as I did to get through college, I was still a couple of courses short of graduating with the rest of my class in 1969. The draft board wouldn't let me go the extra semester to finish college—they said, "That's it—you've had your four years." I did everything I could to delay it, transferring [draft] boards—everyone knew all these tricks for delaying—from suburban Chicago to the Virginia suburbs of Washington. That got me another month or two, and eventually they said, "It's time for your physical." I was still trying to stay in college, still trying to get my courses done; but it just collapsed around Christmas 1969.

I proposed to my girlfriend, saying, "Why don't we go live in Canada?" That was more than she could handle. I lost my girl. The college career had come to an end with the draft. I had no work at that point. I decided to go to Canada.

I reserved a flight from O'Hare Airport in Chicago to Toronto via Air Canada, under a different name. Once at O'Hare, I went immediately up to the hundred-thousand-mile club and hid out up there until the very last minute, then rushed down to catch the flight. An hour and a half later, we were landing in Toronto. . . .

Everywhere I went for work in Toronto was an American subsidiary, and there was no way they were going to hire me. The strictly Canadian firms didn't want an immigrant. This went on for about three months. I got very sick and nearly died. I finally decided to move to

Vancouver to be closer to my girlfriend in San Francisco. . . .

With my landed immigrant status, I could look for work. Two months later, I found a job as a dishwasher in a hospital, at a dollar thirty-five an hour. I moved up to gardener. Later I helped reorganize an insurance agency, started getting into my old line of work, managing and consulting on organization.

There was constant harassment of my family by the FBI—they knew damn well I was in Vancouver, but they would arrive at my family's house at two and three A.M. and bang on the door and wake them up and demand to see whether or not I was living there. They did that for years. My family didn't even tell me about it for a year or two, they were so embarrassed by it.

I drove down to San Francisco in 1970 to visit my girlfriend and stayed in California for a few days. While I was there, someone came to the door who looked like a narc, which got everyone suspicious. Two hours later, the police arrived suddenly from all directions and completely surrounded the building. I ran from the apartment, up the stairs to the roof, to escape. The worst thing about being a draft dodger is the dreams that you have for years of being chased. It turned out to be a false fire alarm for the building across the street. The next day, I went back to Vancouver.

Sherry Gershon Gottlieb, ed., *Hell No We Won't Go: Resisting the Draft During the Vietnam War.* New York: Viking, 1991.

Veterans Call for an End to the War

For five days in mid-April 1971, a group of Vietnam veterans took part in one of the most highly publicized antiwar demonstrations in the Vietnam era. Among a crowd of nearly 200,000 protesters, 1,100 discharged vets—organized as the Vietnam Veterans Against the War (VVAW)—came to Washington, D.C., to lobby Congress to end America's conflicts in Southeast Asia. On April 23, the last day of the rally, the veterans threw their war medals on the steps of the Capitol building in symbolic protest.

John Kerry was the spokesman for the VVAW. The day before the tossing of the medals, Kerry testified before the Senate Foreign Relations Committee. In his statement, Kerry argued that American politicians were comfortably distanced from the atrocities that he and other veterans had committed on behalf of the government. Kerry expressed regret for his duty in Vietnam, insisting the government was betraying its military personnel by waging a war that had no moral purpose. John Kerry would later enter politics, becoming a Senator for Massachusetts in 1984.

Each day to facilitate the process by which the United States washes her hands of Vietnam someone has to give up his life so that the United States doesn't have to admit something that the entire world already knows, so that we can't say that we have made a mistake. Someone has to die so that President Nixon won't be, and these are his words, "the first President to lose a war."

We are asking Americans to think about that because how do you ask a man to be the last man to die in Vietnam? How do you ask a man to be the last man to die for a mistake? But we are trying to do that, and we are doing it with thousands of rationalizations, and if you read carefully the President's last speech to the people of this country, you can see that he says, and says clearly, "but the issue, gentlemen, the issue, is communism, and the question is whether or not we will leave that country to the communists or whether or not we will try to give it hope to be a free people." But the point is they are not a free people now under us. They are not a free people, and we cannot fight communism all over the world. I think we should have learned that lesson by now. . . .

We are asking here in Washington for some action; action from the Congress of the United States of America which has the

power to raise and maintain armies, and which by the Constitution also has the power to declare war.

We have come here, not to the President, because we believe that this body can be responsive to the will of the people, and we believe that the will of the

Vietnam veterans litter the White House lawn with medals and honors in protest of the war.

people says that we should be out of Vietnam now.

We are here in Washington also to say that the problem of this war is not just a question of war and diplomacy. It is part and parcel of everything that we are trying as human beings to communicate to people in this country—the question of racism which is rampant in the military, and so many other questions such as the use of weapons; the hypocrisy in our taking umbrage at the Geneva Conventions and using that as justification for a continuation of this war when we are more guilty than any other body of violations of those Geneva Conventions; in the use of free fire zones, harassment interdiction fire, search and destroy missions, the bombings, the torture of prisoners, the killing of prisoners, all accepted policy by many units in South Vietnam. That

is what we are trying to say. It is part and parcel of everything. . . .

We are also here to ask, and we are here to ask vehemently, where are the leaders of our country? Where is the leadership? We are here to ask where are McNamara, Rostow, Bundy, Gilpatrick and so many others? Where are they now that we, the men whom they sent off to war, have returned? These are commanders who have deserted their troops, and there is no more serious crime in the laws of war. The Army says they never leave their wounded. The Marines say they never leave even their dead. These men have left all the casualties and retreated behind a pious shield of public rectitude. They have left the real stuff of their reputations bleaching behind them in the sun in this country.

John Kerry, Statement Before the U.S. Senate Committee on Foreign Relations, April 22, 1971.

Chapter 4

Pulling Out

In January 1968, the North Vietnamese Army (NVA) launched a coordinated strike with the Viet Cong (VC) against cities and military bases throughout South Vietnam. The attacks fell on the Vietnamese holiday of Tet and caught most South Vietnamese civilians and U.S. servicemen by surprise. The U.S. military had been winning all of its major engagements with the enemy and did not expect that the NVA or VC had the capabilities to launch an invasion of the South. More profoundly, however, the offensive shocked Americans at home. Despite the warning cries of war protesters, many average Americans believed U.S. troops were winning the war. The news of the Tet Offensive revealed otherwise. Obviously, the Communist forces still had incredible will and could seemingly strike anywhere in South Vietnam.

In response to the Tet Offensive, General Earle Wheeler, chairman of the joint chiefs of staff, asked President Lyndon B.

Johnson to commit another 200,000 troops to Vietnam. Johnson begged off for a time, insisting that he would first appoint a counsel to review America's involvement. This advisory body returned their verdict in March, cautioning the president against further troop deployments. With antiwar sentiment running high in the nation and his staff pointing out the pitfalls of escalation, President Johnson broadcast a televised speech in which he announced he would halt the bombing campaign over North Vietnam and initiate peace talks with the government in Hanoi. He also revealed that he would not run for another term as president. The national disunity engendered by the war had clearly broken the will of the president who had first sent troops to fight in Vietnam.

With peace talks supposedly underway, the American people felt that perhaps an end to the war may be close at hand. Their confidence was bolstered when

Johnson's successor, Richard M. Nixon, instituted the first of many U.S. troop withdrawals in May 1969. Nixon's overall plan was to pull U.S. soldiers out of the conflict and replace them with South Vietnamese forces. "Vietnamization" was the name given to Nixon's strategy. By pledging continued support of the South Vietnam military, Nixon believed he could get American soldiers out of harm's way while saving the nation's reputation as a sponsor of democratic governments.

To the antiwar factions in the United States, however, Nixon's actions fell short of ending U.S. involvement. And in April 1970, the nation learned that Nixon had ordered American troops in Vietnam to cross the border into Cambodia to attack Viet Cong bases there. Many of the administration's opponents believed this move was both illegal (since the United States had not declared war on Cambodia) and an indication that the president was widening the war, not bringing it to a close. Even Congress seemed hostile to the president's wanton abuse of power. At the onset of 1971, Congress forbade the further use of U.S. troops in Cambodia or other Southeast Asian states.

Despite appearances that the president might be going back on his pledge to garner peace, Nixon was still decreasing the

Vietnamese civilians sort through the wreckage of their homes after the bombings of the Tet Offensive.

number of troops stationed in Vietnam. By December 1971, only 157,000 military personnel remained in Vietnam from the 1969 peak level of 543,000. Furthermore, throughout his administration, Nixon was carrying on peace negotiations with the government of North Vietnam. National Security Adviser Henry Kissinger was making all sorts of secret concessions (unbeknownst to the American public) to bring Hanoi to agreeable terms. However, at meetings in Paris, Kissinger seemed to make headway only to have one side or the other reject the conditions of peace. In December 1972, Nixon even reinstated the bombing of North Vietnam in an effort to force Hanoi into relaxing its stringent demands at the bargaining table. But the United States was arguing from a position of weakness. By then only around 25,000 U.S. troops remained in Vietnam, and the South Vietnamese defense forces were failing to stem the advancing army of the North.

In January 1973, the Paris Peace Accords were finally signed, and the United States promised to remove its remaining forces within sixty days. Although Nixon made good on his word, he fully intended to continue to sponsor the South Vietnamese military. And South Vietnam's president, Nguyen Van Thieu, believed the United States would not let South Vietnam fall to Communists regardless of a treaty. As American troops withdrew, President Thieu violated the accords by sending South Vietnamese troops into regions that both North and South claimed to control. The fighting recommenced, and Thieu found that his faith in the United States was unsubstantiated. Nixon resigned in August 1974, and his successor, Gerald R. Ford, was unable to convince Congress to supply more aid to South Vietnam. The Communist forces overran the South in less than a year. Decrying American betrayal, Thieu resigned in April 1975, just days before the capital of Saigon fell to the victorious North.

An Optimistic View of the Tet Offensive

The massiveness of the 1968 Tet Offensive caused fear both in U.S. servicemen in the field and Americans at home. While many people in the United States had believed America was winning the war, the Tet Offensive proved that South Vietnam was still far from secure. To shore up public confidence in the government's pursuit of victory in Vietnam, Secretary of Defense Robert S. McNamara insisted that the North Vietnamese Army and Viet Cong had suffered many casualties while failing to achieve their objectives during the Tet Offensive. Although technically McNamara was correct in arguing that the U.S. military thwarted the Communist invasion, he was hard pressed to convince the American public that the Tet Offensive was a U.S. victory. Still, as in this television interview

During a press conference Robert McNamara (right) and President Johnson attempt to convince the public that Tet was an American victory.

from February 4, McNamara maintained his optimism.

Question: Mr. Secretary, are you telling us the fact that the Viet Cong, after all these years, were able to, temporarily at least, grab control of some 20-odd Provincial capitals and the city of Saigon—are you telling us this has no military meaning at all?

Secretary McNamara: No; certainly not. I think South Viet-Nam is such a complex situation—one must always look at the pluses and the minuses, and I don't mean to say there haven't been any minuses for the South Vietnamese in the last several days. I think there have been, but there have been many, many pluses. The North Vietnamese and the Viet Cong have not accomplished either one of their major objectives: either to ignite a general uprising or to force a diversion of the troops which the South Vietnamese and the United States have moved into the northern areas of South Viet-Nam, anticipating a major Viet Cong and North Vietnamese offensive in that area.

And beyond that, the North Vietnamese and the Viet Cong have suffered very heavy penalties in terms of losses of weapons and losses of men in the past several days. They have, of course, dealt a very heavy blow to many of the cities of South Viet-Nam.

Robert McNamara, Television Interview, February 4, 1968.

No Prospect of Victory

The Tet Offensive was psychologically damaging to the U.S. war effort. The daring and bravado of the assault made many supporters of the war reconsider their position. The U.S. military was clearly not in control of South Vietnam and had not robbed the North of its means or its will to continue the fight. Americans now understood the war could conceivably go on for many more years.

Senator Robert F. Kennedy was an outspoken critic of prolonging U.S. involvement in Vietnam. Although once in favor of the war, by 1967 Kennedy recognized that the government had no decisive plan for winning and bringing the struggle to an end. In a February 8, 1968, speech, Kennedy urged Americans to rid themselves of the illusion that the United States was close to victory in Vietnam.

Our enemy, savagely striking at will across all of South Vietnam, has finally shattered the mask of official illusion with which we have concealed our true circumstances, even from ourselves. But a short time ago we were serene in our reports and predictions of progress.

The Viet Cong will probably withdraw from the cities, as they were forced to withdraw from the American Embassy [in Saigon, which they temporarily occupied]. Thousands of them will be dead. But they will, nevertheless, have demonstrated that no part or person of South Vietnam is secure from their attacks: neither district capitals nor American bases, neither the peasant in his rice paddy nor the commanding general of our own great forces. . . .

The events of the last two weeks have taught us something. For the sake of those young Americans who are fighting today, if for no other reason, the time has come to take a new look at the war in Vietnam; not by cursing the past but by using it to illuminate the future. . . .

We must, first of all, rid ourselves of the illusion that the events of the past two weeks represent some sort of victory. That is not so. It is said the Viet Cong will not be able to hold the cities. This is probably true. But they have demonstrated despite all our reports of progress, of government strength and enemy weakness, that half a million American soldiers with 700,000 Vietnamese allies, with total command of the air, total command of the sea, backed by huge resources and the most modern weapons, are unable to secure even a single city from the attacks of an enemy whose total strength is about 250,000. . . .

For years we have been told that the measure of our success and progress in Vietnam was increasing security and control for the population. Now we have seen that none of the population is secure and no area is under sure control. . . .

This has not happened because our men are not brave or effective, because they are. It is because we have misconceived the nature of the war. It is because we have sought to resolve by military might a conflict whose issue depends upon the will and conviction of the South Vietnamese people. It is like sending a lion to halt an epidemic of jungle rot [skin infection common among soldiers in Vietnam].

This misconception rests on a second illusion—the illusion that we can win a war which the South Vietnamese cannot win for themselves. You cannot expect people to risk their lives and endure hardship unless they have a stake in their own society. They must have a clear sense of identification with their own government, a belief they are participating in a cause worth fighting for. People will not fight to line the pockets of generals or swell the bank accounts of the wealthy. They are far more likely to close their eyes and shut their doors in

the face of the government—even as they did last week.

More than any election, more than any proud boast, that single fact reveals the truth. We have an ally in name only. We support a government without supporters. Without the efforts of American arms that government would not last a day.

The third illusion is that the unswerving pursuit of military victory, whatever its

Senator Robert F. Kennedy speaks out against President Johnson's Vietnam policies.

cost, is in the interest of either ourselves or the people of Vietnam. For the people of Vietnam, the last three years have meant little but horror. Their tiny land has been devastated by a weight of bombs and shells greater than Nazi Germany knew in the Second World War. . . .

Whatever the outcome of these battles, it is the people we seek to defend who are the greatest losers. . . .

The fourth illusion is that the American national interest is identical with—or should be subordinated to—the selfish interest of an incompetent military regime. . . . The fifth illusion is that this war can be settled in our own way and in our own time on our own terms. Such a settlement is the privilege of the triumphant: of those who crush their enemies in battle or wear away their will to fight. We have not done this, nor is there any prospect we will achieve such a victory.

Unable to defeat our enemy or break his will—at least without a huge, long and ever more costly effort—we must actively seek a peaceful settlement. . . .

No war has ever demanded more bravery from our people and our government—not just bravery under fire or the bravery to make sacrifices—but the bravery to discard the comfort of illusion—to do away with false hopes and alluring promises. . . .

This is a great nation and a strong people. Any who seek to comfort rather than speak plainly, reassure rather than instruct, promise satisfaction rather than

reveal frustration—they deny that greatness and drain that strength. For today as it was in the beginning, it is the truth that makes us free.

Robert F. Kennedy, Speech on the Vietnam War, February 8, 1968.

Stalemate

Media coverage of the Vietnam War had a great impact on shaping the attitudes of the American public. Print journalists provided editorials on U.S. involvement while television broadcast images of battle as well as nightly death tolls of soldiers killed in action. Although many have argued that the prevalence of images and reports roused public sentiment against the war, not all news media was critical of government policy. Even when the protest movement garnered television coverage, many reporters were antagonistic to the demonstrators. The conflicting views left the average American undecided. Yet the public looked to the news media for facts and opinions.

Walter Cronkite was a respected anchorman for the CBS Evening News *during the Vietnam era. He had been a war correspondent in World War II. Cronkite had earned a reputation as a clear-thinking, patriotic journalist, and people trusted his views. In February 1968, he traveled to South Vietnam in the wake of the Tet Offensive. Hoping to find that the government assurances of a coming victory were true, Cronkite was dismayed by the disheveled military structure and unstable political situation in the South. On February 27, the respected journalist aired his newfound impressions to the CBS audience. During the broadcast a grim Cronkite made it clear that despite the official boasts of impending U.S. victory, the situation in Vietnam could at best be described as a costly stalemate. In retrospect, critics of the era claim that Cronkite's broadcast may have done more to turn public opinion against the war than all the antiwar protests combined.*

There are doubts about the measure of success or setback, but even more, there are doubts about the exact measure of the disaster itself. All that is known with certainty is that on the first two nights of the Tet Lunar New Year, the Viet Cong and North Vietnamese Regular Forces, violating the truce agreed on for that holiday, struck across the entire length of South Vietnam, hitting the largest thirty-five cities, towns, and provincial capitals. How many died and how much damage was done, however, are still but approximations, despite the official figures. . . .

We'd like to sum up our findings in Vietnam, an analysis that must be speculative, personal, subjective. Who won and who lost in the great Tet Offensive against the cities? I'm not sure. The Viet Cong did not win by a knockout, but neither did we. The referees of history may make it a draw. Another stand-off may be coming in the big battles expected south of the Demilitarized Zone [DMZ]. Khe

Sanh [U.S. Marine Corps base] could well fall, with a terrible loss in American lives, prestige, and morale, and this is a tragedy of our stubbornness there; but the bastion no longer is a key to the rest of the northern regions, and it is doubtful that the American forces can be defeated across the breadth of the DMZ with any substantial loss of ground. Another stand-off. On the political front, past performance gives no confidence that the Vietnamese government can cope with its problems, now compounded by the attack on the cities. It may not fall, it may hold on, but it probably won't show the dynamic qualities demanded of this young nation. Another stand-off.

We have been too often disappointed by the optimism of the American leaders, both in Vietnam and Washington, to have faith any longer in the silver linings they find in the darkest clouds. They may be right, that Hanoi's winter-spring offensive had been forced by the Communist realization that they could not win the longer war of attrition, and that the Communists hope that any success in the offensive will improve their position for eventual negotiations. It would improve their position, and it would also require our realization, that we should have had all along, that any negotiations must be that—negotiations, not the dictation of peace terms. For it seems now more certain than ever that the bloody experience of Vietnam is to end in a stalemate.

This summer's almost certain stand-off will either end in real give-and-take negotiations or terrible escalation; and for every means we have to escalate, the enemy can match us, and that applies to invasion of the North, the use of nuclear weapons, or the mere commitment of 100-, or 200-, or 300,000 more American troops to the battle. And with each escalation, the world comes closer to the brink of cosmic disaster.

To say that we are closer to victory today is to believe, in the face of the evidence, the optimists who have been wrong in the past. To suggest we are on the edge of defeat is to yield to unreasonable pessimism. To say that we are mired in stalemate seems the only realistic, yet unsatisfactory, conclusion. On the off chance that military and political analysts are right, in the next few months we must test the enemy's intentions, in case this is indeed his last gasp before negotiations. But it is increasingly clear to this reporter that the only rational way out then will be to negotiate, not as victors, but as an honorable people who lived up to their pledge to defend democracy, and did the best they could.

Walter Cronkite, Broadcast on CBS Television, February 27, 1968.

Johnson De-Escalates the War

With antiwar sentiment running high following the surprise Tet Offensive, President Lyndon Johnson felt the pressure to change his policies toward Vietnam. In a televised address, a deflated Johnson told the nation that he was taking initial steps to de-escalate the war in hopes that a peaceful settlement to the conflict could be found. While this announcement was momentous on its own, Johnson followed it with the shocking statement that he would not seek reelection in the coming presidential race. Many viewers understood the president's agony but hoped that America could finally close the book on the Vietnam War. They were soon to learn that the United States had only turned yet another chapter in the continuing conflict.

Tonight I want to speak to you of peace in Vietnam and Southeast Asia.

No other question so preoccupies our people. No other dream so absorbs the 250 million human beings who live in that part of the world. No other goal motivates American policy in Southeast Asia. . . .

Tonight, I renew the offer I made last August—to stop the bombardment of North Vietnam. We ask that talks begin promptly, that they be serious talks on the substance of peace. We assume that during those talks Hanoi will not take advantage of our restraint.

We are prepared to move immediately toward peace through negotiations.

So, tonight, in hope that this action will lead to early talks, I am taking the first step to deescalate the conflict. We are reducing—substantially reducing—the present level of hostilities.

And we are doing so unilaterally, and at once. . . .

I believe that a peaceful Asia is far nearer to reality because of what America has done in Vietnam. I believe that the men who endure the dangers of battle—fighting there for us tonight—are helping the entire world avoid far greater conflicts, far wider wars, far more destruction, than this one.

The peace that will bring them home someday will come. Tonight I have offered the first in what I hope will be a series of mutual moves toward peace.

I pray that it will not be rejected by the leaders of North Vietnam. I pray that they will accept it as a means by which the sacrifices of their own people may be ended. And I ask your help and your support, my fellow citizens, for this effort to reach across the battlefield toward an early peace. . . .

Fifty-two months and 10 days ago, in a moment of tragedy and trauma, the duties of this office fell upon me. I asked then for your help and God's, that we might continue America on its course, binding up our wounds, healing our history, moving forward in new unity, to clear the American agenda and to keep the American commitment for all of our people.

United we have kept that commitment. United we have enlarged that commitment.

Through all time to come, I think America will be a stronger nation, a more just society, and a land of greater opportunity and fulfillment because of what we have done together in these years of unparalleled achievement.

Our reward will come in the life of freedom, peace, and hope that our children will enjoy through ages ahead.

What we won when all of our people united just must not now be lost in suspicion, distrust, selfishness, and politics among any of our people.

Believing this as I do, I have concluded that I should not permit the Presidency to become involved in the partisan divisions that are developing in this political year.

With America's sons in the fields far away, with America's future under challenge right here at home, with our hopes and the world's hopes for peace in the balance every day, I do not believe that I should devote an hour or a day of my time to any personal partisan causes or to any duties other than the awesome duties of this office—the Presidency of your country.

Accordingly, I shall not seek, and I will not accept, the nomination of my party for another term as your President.

But let men everywhere know, however, that a strong, a confident, and a vigilant America stands ready tonight to seek an honorable peace—and stands ready tonight to defend an honored cause—whatever the price, whatever the burden, whatever the sacrifice that duty may require.

Thank you for listening.

Good night and God bless all of you.

Lyndon Johnson, "The President's Address to the Nation Announcing Steps to Limit the War in Vietnam and Reporting His Decision Not to Seek Re-Election," March 31, 1968.

To End the War by Winning the Peace

Soon after Lyndon Johnson initiated his program to de-escalate the Vietnam War, his successor, Richard Nixon, took office. The new president was not willing to be bullied into a quick negotiation of peace with North Vietnam. Instead he proposed a plan to gradually turn the brunt of the fighting back over to South Vietnam's military while opening communication with the Hanoi government. In June 1969, Nixon began withdrawing U.S. troops from combat and replacing them with South Vietnamese forces. His gesture, however, did not appease the anti-war factions who wanted immediate withdrawal of all U.S. personnel. In October, massive demonstrations were staged in cities across the nation. In response, a resentful Nixon aired a televised address on November 3 in which he claimed that the silent majority of Americans should support his plan. Even if it would prolong the fighting, Nixon assured the nation that although America might lose the war it would win the peace.

Tonight I want to talk to you on a subject of deep concern to all Americans and to many people in all parts of the world—the war in Vietnam. . . .

Three American Presidents have recognized the great stakes involved in Vietnam and understood what had to be done.

In 1963, President Kennedy, with his characteristic eloquence and clarity, said: "we want to see a stable government there, carrying on a struggle to maintain its national independence."

"We believe strongly in that. We are not going to withdraw from that effort. In my opinion, for us to withdraw from that effort would mean a collapse not only of South Viet-Nam, but Southeast Asia. So we are going to stay there."

President Eisenhower and President Johnson expressed the same conclusion during their terms of office.

For the future of peace, precipitate withdrawal would thus be a disaster of immense magnitude.

—A nation cannot remain great if it betrays its allies and lets down its friends.

—Our defeat and humiliation in South Vietnam without question would promote recklessness in the councils of those great powers who have not yet abandoned their goals of world conquest.

—This would spark violence wherever our commitments help maintain the peace—in the Middle East, in Berlin, eventually even in the Western Hemisphere.

Soldiers board the USS Revere, *bound for home, after President Richard Nixon begins withdrawing troops from Vietnam.*

Ultimately, this would cost more lives.

It would not bring peace; it would bring more war. . . .

In speaking of the consequences of a precipitate withdrawal, I mentioned that our allies would lose confidence in America.

Far more dangerous, we would lose confidence in ourselves. Oh, the immediate reaction would be a sense of relief that our men were coming home. But as we saw the consequences of what we had done, inevitable remorse and divisive recrimination would scar our spirit as a people. . . .

Two hundred years ago this nation was weak and poor. But even then, America was the hope of millions in the world. Today we have become the strongest and richest nation in the world. And the wheel of destiny has turned so that any hope the world has for the survival of peace and freedom will be determined by whether the American people have the moral stamina and the courage to meet the challenge of free world leadership.

Let historians not record that when America was the most powerful nation in the world we passed on the other side of the road and allowed the last hopes for peace and freedom of millions of people to be suffocated by the forces of totalitarianism.

And so tonight—to you, the great silent majority of my fellow Americans—I ask for your support.

I pledged in my campaign for the Presidency to end the war in a way that we could win the peace. I have initiated a plan of action which will enable me to keep that pledge.

The more support I can have from the American people, the sooner that pledge can be redeemed; for the more divided we are at home, the less likely the enemy is to negotiate at Paris.

Let us be united for peace. Let us also be united against defeat. Because let us understand: North Vietnam cannot defeat or humiliate the United States. Only Americans can do that. . . .

Thank you and goodnight.

Richard M. Nixon, Address to the Nation on the War in Vietnam, November 3, 1969.

Crossing into Cambodia

In April 1970, U.S. troops crossed the South Vietnam border and entered Cambodia. Their mission was to destroy base camps the Viet Cong had set up in that neutral nation. Believing the action was justified in pursuing Communist forces, the Nixon administration had not sought permission to enter the sovereign land. In fact, the president had not even informed Congress of the maneuver. President Nixon tried to keep the border incursions a secret since he was not willing to declare war on Cambodia and suffer the public backlash. But the invasion was too large to hide for long. At the end of the month, Nixon issued a televised address to explain why he had taken the initiative to enter Cambodia. In his defense, he argued the action was to protect U.S. soldiers in Vietnam. He also claimed that this was the first time the United States had violated Cambodian borders.

American reaction to the controversial invasion was immediate. In one debate, five Congressmen asked George McT. Kahin, a political science professor at Cornell University, to respond to Nixon's claims. Kahin contradicted the president's statements by reading evidence of previous incursions into Cambodia and neighboring Laos. He warned that the administration had acted rashly and risked greater involvement in Southeast Asia.

Referring to Vietnamese communist sanctuaries in Cambodia, President Nixon stated on April 30: "For five years neither the U.S. nor South Vietnam moved against those enemy sanctuaries because we did not wish to violate the territory of a neutral nation."

The Historical Record

In July 1965 the International Control Commission (I.C.C.) reported on evidence of border crossings into Cambodia by South Vietnamese forces, stating that there were 375 such incidents in 1964 and 385 in the first five months of 1965 alone. The commission unanimously concluded that "None of those incidents were provoked by the Royal Government of Cambodia." From that time on there were repeated reports of border incursions and air attacks against border areas inside Cambodia chiefly by South Vietnamese but also by American forces. . . .

On January 22, 1968, the U.S. acknowledged that a U.S.–South Vietnamese patrol had made a limited intrusion into Cambodia following fire from Vietnamese communist units on the Cambodian side. (NYT [*New York Times*] January 23, 1968)

In April 1969, U.S. air and artillery attacks were launched against communist bases inside Cambodia. (NYT April 26, 1969)

On May 8, 1969, U.S. B-52 bombers raided communist supply dumps and camps within Cambodia. (NYT May 9, 1969)

October–December, 1969, [Cambodia's monarch, Prince Norodom] Sihanouk protested continuing U.S. bombing of Cambodian border areas. . . .

If, as the Administration has repeatedly stated, the Vietnamization program was designed to reduce American commitments in Southeast Asia and to facilitate the achievement of a negotiated settlement of the war, the Cambodian adventure is impossible to justify. By enlarging the area of conflict and the scope of American commitments and by increasing the number of disputing parties, it adds enormously to the length and complexity of any agenda for negotiations. With the U.S. and the Vietnamese now enmeshed in a Cambodian civil war a virtually insoluble Cambodian problem is added to the already intractable Vietnamese problem. It is no longer enough to settle the war in Vietnam and Laos; we are assuming a responsibility for settling a Cambodian war as well.

George McT. Kahin, *Cambodia: The Administration's Version and the Historical Record.* Ithaca, NY: Glad Day Press, 1970.

Coming Home

As servicemen finished their tour of duty or were withdrawn under Nixon's plan, they were faced with the thought of going back home. Most soldiers were elated at the prospect of returning to loved ones and escaping the unpopular war. Peter Roepcke was rotated out of Vietnam in mid-1970 after sustaining an injury. On April 20, he wrote home of his impending return. Amid his expressions of joy and relief, however, Roepcke relates some of the horrifying images that will doubtlessly haunt him for life.

After returning to the United States, many veterans had a difficult time adjust-

Soldiers board a carrier plane for home, where they will face the contempt of antiwar demonstrators.

ing to their old lives. Unlike in previous wars, there were no parades or public celebrations for Vietnam vets. Often they were greeted by derisive crowds of antiwar demonstrators who accused the servicemen of perpetuating murder in Vietnam. The scars of battle coupled with the lackluster welcome left many Vietnam veterans feeling like outsiders to a society that seemed to want to forget them and all reminders of the war.

Hi doll,

I don't know who will get home first, me or this letter. But I thought I would write anyway. It was so good to hear your voice [last night]. The connections were weak, but still the same you sounded great. I can still hear you saying, "I can't believe it." You sounded so happy, and it sounded like you did not believe that I only busted a few bones.

I got a call through to my parents a little while after I talked to you. My mother did not believe that I was coming home. But I finally got through to her. And, boy, was she happy. She said she was sorry that I got hurt, but also glad—you know, glad that it was only this and not something worse.

You don't know how close I have been to getting killed or maimed. Too many times I have seen guys near me get hit and go home in a plastic bag. Like I have said before, someone was looking over me.

Well, it is all over now. Now it's time to forget. But it's hard to forget these things. I close my eyes and try to sleep, but all I can see is Jenkins lying there with his brains hanging out or Lefty with his eyes shot out. You know these guys—we have lived with them for a long time. We know their wives or girlfriends. Then you stop to think it could be me. Hell, I don't know why I am writing all this. But it feels better getting it out of my mind.

So, doll, in titi [a short] time I will be with you again. . . .

Well, honey, I will close for now. Until I see you again,

I love you.

Yours,

Pete

Bernard Edelman, ed. *Dear America: Letters Home from Vietnam.* New York: Pocket Books, 1986.

Demoralization of the Military

By the early 1970s the morale of the U.S. fighting forces in Vietnam was at an un-

precedented low. The soldiers knew they were fighting an unpopular war, and they also sensed that with the steady withdrawal of troops, they would be home soon. With these incentives, many soldiers did everything they could to avoid engaging the enemy. No one wanted to be the last serviceman to die in Vietnam. In a June 1971 article for Armed Forces Journal, *reporter Robert D. Heinl Jr. addressed the issue of demoralization, pointing out all the contributing factors that placed the army on the verge of collapse.*

The morale, discipline and battleworthiness of the U.S. Armed Forces are, with a few salient exceptions, lower and worse than at any time in this century and possibly in the history of the United States.

By every conceivable indicator, our army that now remains in Vietnam is in a state approaching collapse, with individual units avoiding or having refused combat, murdering their officers and noncommissioned officers, drug-ridden, and dispirited where not near-mutinous.

Elsewhere than Vietnam, the situation is nearly as serious.

Intolerably clobbered and buffeted from without and within by social turbulence, pandemic drug addiction, race war, sedition, civilian scapegoatise, draftee recalcitrance and malevolence, barracks theft and common crime, unsupported in their travail by the general government, in Congress as well as the executive branch, distrusted, disliked, and often reviled by the public, the uniformed services today are places of agony for the loyal, silent professionals who doggedly hang on and try to keep the ship afloat.

The responses of the services of these unheard-of conditions, forces and new public attitudes, are confused, resentful, occasionally pollyanna-ish, and in some cases even calculated to worsen the malaise that is wracking them. . . .

To understand the military consequences of what is happening to the U.S. Armed Forces, Vietnam is a good place to start. It is in Vietnam that the rearguard of a 500,000-man army, in its day (and in the observation of the writer) the best army the United States ever put into the field, is numbly extricating itself from a nightmare war the Armed Forces feel they had foisted on them by bright civilians who are now back on campus writing books about the folly of it all.

"They have set up separate companies," writes an American soldier from Cu Chi, quoted in the New York Times, "for men who refuse to go out into the field." It is no big thing to refuse to go. If a man is ordered to go to such and such a place he no longer goes through the hassle of refusing; he just packs his shirt and goes to visit some buddies at another base camp. Operations have become incredibly ragtag. Many guys don't even put on their uniforms any more. . . .

"Frag incidents" or just "fragging" is current soldier slang in Vietnam for the murder or attempted murder of strict, unpopular, or just aggressive officers and NCOs [Non-commissioned Officers]. With extreme reluctance (after a young West Pointer from Senator Mike Mansfield's Montana was fragged in his sleep) the Pentagon has now disclosed that fraggings in 1970 (209) have more than doubled those of the previous year (96). . . .

The issue of "combat refusal," an official euphemism for disobedience of orders to fight—the soldier's gravest crime—has only recently been again precipitated on the frontier of Laos by Troop B, 1st Cavalry's mass refusal to recapture their captain's command vehicle containing communication gear, codes and other secret operation orders. . . .

"Search and evade" (meaning tacit avoidance of combat by units in the field) is now virtually a principle of war, vividly expressed by the GI phrase, "CYA (cover your ass) and get home!"

That "search-and-evade" has not gone unnoticed by the enemy is underscored by the Viet Cong delegation's recent statement at the Paris Peace Talks that communist units in Indochina have been ordered not to engage American units which do not molest them. The same statement boasted—not without foundation in fact—that American defectors are in the VC ranks. . . .

As for drugs and race, Vietnam's problems today not only reflect but reinforce those of the Armed Forces as a whole. In April, for example, members of a Congressional investigating subcommittee reported that 10 to 15% of our troops in Vietnam are now using high-grade heroin, and that drug addiction there is "of epidemic proportions.". . .

It is a truism that national armies closely reflect societies from which they have been raised. It would be strange indeed if the Armed Forces did not today mirror the agonizing divisions and social traumas of American society, and of course they do.

For this very reason, our Armed Forces outside Vietnam not only reflect these conditions but disclose the depths of their troubles in an awful litany of sedition, disaffection, desertion, race, drugs, breakdowns of authority, abandonment of discipline, and, as a cumulative result, the lowest state of military morale in the history of the country.

Robert D. Heinl Jr., "The Collapse of the Armed Forces," *Armed Forces Journal,* June 7, 1971.

After a long, demoralizing war, Henry Kissinger (lower left) and Vietnamese ambassadors initiate the Paris Peace Accords.

An Unstable Peace

Peace negotiations involving the United States, South Vietnam, and North Vietnam had stalled by the time President Nixon took office in 1969. In an attempt to move things forward, Nixon dispatched National Security Adviser Henry Kissinger to offer concessions to the North. The meetings were held in secret and the U.S. public had no knowledge of the terms being offered. Despite Kissinger's declaration that "peace was at hand," the negotiations fell through and all parties left disgruntled. Kissinger reopened talks the following year, but with much the same results. In frustration, Nixon ordered U.S. warplanes to bomb Hanoi in hopes that the government of North Vietnam would yield some concessions in future peace talks. The strategy failed, and Kissinger met with Hanoi representatives who were determined the United Stated would meet their demands. Eventually, a peace agreement was worked out in Paris and signed by the opposing sides on January 27, 1973. Three days previously, when all parties had agreed to the terms, President Nixon gave a national address to announce the official end to America's involvement in Vietnam. Yet even as peace was declared, none of the parties intended to adhere to the agreement. Each side accused the other of violating the treaty and the fighting continued. Only 24,000 U.S. troops remained in Vietnam at the time the Paris Peace Accords were signed, and these would be withdrawn in March. But Nixon continued to bolster the South Vietnamese military machine which violated the cease-fire agreements of the treaty. With American support, the South Vietnamese fought on—though in a losing battle—for two more years.

Good evening. I have asked for this radio and television time tonight for the purpose of announcing that we today have concluded an agreement to end the war and bring peace with honor in Vietnam and Southeast Asia.

The following statement is being issued at this moment in Washington and Hanoi:

"At 12:30 Paris time today, Jan. 23, 1973, the agreement on ending the war and restoring peace in Vietnam was initialed by Dr. Henry Kissinger on behalf of the United States and Special Adviser Le Duc Tho on behalf of the Democratic Republic of Vietnam.

"The agreement will be formally signed by the parties participating in the Paris Conference on Vietnam on Jan. 27, 1973, at the International Conference Center in Paris. The cease-fire will take effect at 2400 Greenwich mean time, Jan. 27, 1973. The United States and the Democratic Republic of Vietnam express the hope that this agreement will insure stable peace in Vietnam and contribute to the preservation of lasting peace in Indochina and Southeast Asia." . . .

As this long and very difficult war ends I would like to address a few special words to each of those who have been parties in the conflict.

First, to the people and Government of South Vietnam. By your courage, by your sacrifice, you have won the precious right to determine your own future and you have developed the strength to defend that right.

We look forward to working with you in the future, friends in peace as we have been allies in war.

To the leaders of North Vietnam: As we have ended the war through negotiations, let us now build a peace of reconciliation.

For our part, we are prepared to make a major effort to help achieve that goal. But just as reciprocity was needed to end the war, so too will it be needed to build and strengthen the peace.

To the other major powers that have been involved, even indirectly: Now is the time for mutual restraint so that the peace we have achieved can last.

And finally, to all of you who are listening, the American people: Your steadfastness in supporting our insistence on peace with honor has made peace with honor possible. . . .

Now that we have achieved an honorable agreement let us be proud that America did not settle for a peace that would have betrayed our allies, that would have abandoned our prisoners of war or that would have ended the war for us but would have continued the war for the 50 million people of Indochina.

Let us be proud of the two and a half million young Americans who served in Vietnam, who served with honor and distinction in one of the most selfless enterprises in the history of nations.

And let us be proud of those who sacrificed, who gave their lives, so that the people of South Vietnam might live in freedom, and so that the world might live in peace.

Richard M. Nixon, "Transcript of the Speech by the President on Vietnam." *New York Times,* January 24, 1973.

☆ Chronology of Events ☆

May 1954

French forces are defeated at Dien Bien Phu.

July 1954

By the Geneva accords, Vietnam is temporarily divided into a Communist North and democratic South pending general elections.

October 1954

President Dwight Eisenhower pledges military support to Ngo Dinh Diem, president of South Vietnam.

April 1956

The last French troops withdraw from Vietnam. U.S. military "advisers" assume the responsibility of training the South Vietnamese forces.

December 1960

North Vietnam supports Communist insurgent forces in South Vietnam (the Viet Cong) in their attempt to overthrow Diem's government.

May 1961

President John F. Kennedy sends U.S. special forces to Vietnam to conduct covert operations against the North.

December 1961

The number of U.S. military personnel in Vietnam tops 3,000. All are advisers and special forces; no combat units have yet been deployed.

November 1963

A military coup ousts Diem from the presidency of South Vietnam. In the United States, President Kennedy is assassinated and Vice President Lyndon Johnson assumes the executive office.

August 1964

American destroyers in the Gulf of Tonkin report that they have been attacked by North Vietnamese vessels. In response, Congress passes the Gulf of Tonkin Resolution.

February 1965

President Johnson authorizes Operation Rolling Thunder, a bombing campaign against North Vietnam. The bombing missions will last for three years.

March 1965

The first 3,500 U.S. Marines land in Da Nang. University faculty at Ann Arbor, Michigan, stage the first "teach-ins" to protest America's policy of aggression in Vietnam.

April 1965

The first mass demonstration against the

war takes place in Washington, D.C.

July 1965

President Johnson escalates the war by increasing the draft call and preparing to send 50,000 more troops to Vietnam.

December 1965

More than 180,000 U.S. military personnel are in Vietnam.

June 1966

Johnson sets new troop levels at 431,000. This will not be reached, however, until the middle of the following year.

June 1967

The protest organization Vietnam Veterans Against the War is formed.

September 1967

After a series of military leaders, South Vietnam elects Nguyen Van Thieu to the presidency.

October 1967

Antiwar demonstrations are held across the United States. President Johnson's approval rating for his handling of the war drops to 28 percent.

January 1968

North Vietnamese forces in coordination with the Viet Cong launch the Tet Offensive. Many South Vietnamese cities are attacked and overrun. After weeks of desperate fighting, the United States regains control of the cities and inflicts severe casualties on the enemy.

February 1968

General Earle Wheeler, chairman of the joint chiefs of staff, asks President Johnson to increase U.S. troops levels by another 206,000. Johnson hesitates, calling upon a special committee to conduct a review of the war before making any decision. In March, the committee cautions against further commitment.

March 1968

Senator Robert F. Kennedy announces he will run for the presidency on the Democratic ticket. President Johnson announces that he will halt the air campaign against the North and will not seek another term as president.

April 1968

Martin Luther King Jr. is assassinated.

May 1968

Peace negotiations between North Vietnam, South Vietnam, and the United States begin in Paris.

June 1968

Robert F. Kennedy is assassinated after winning the California primary.

August 1968

Republican presidential candidate Richard M. Nixon runs on a platform that promises an honorable peace in Vietnam.

November 1968

Richard Nixon wins the presidential election.

June 1969

Nixon orders the removal of 25,000 troops from Vietnam and pledges continued withdrawal. This is part of his overall plan of "Vietnamization," turning the brunt of the fighting over to South Vietnamese forces.

September 1969

Communist leader Ho Chi Minh dies at age seventy-nine.

Novemebr 1969

President Nixon addresses the "silent majority" of Americans who he believes still support his plan for gradual withdrawal from Vietnam. The largest anti-war demonstration to date (attracting some 250,000 people) takes place in Washington, D.C.

April 1970

Nixon authorizes U.S. forces to cross the Vietnamese border and stage raids against Viet Cong bases in Cambodia.

May 1970

National Guardsmen fire into a crowd of students protesting at Kent State University in Ohio. Four students are killed.

December 1970

After a few withdrawals, 335,000 U.S. troops remain in Vietnam.

May 1971

National Security Adviser Henry Kissinger secretly promises North Vietnam that the Unted States will pull all troops out of Vietnam in exchange for the return of all U.S. servicemen held as prisoners of war.

December 1971

The number of U.S. troops in Vietnam falls to 157,000.

May 1972

After failed negotiations with the North, Nixon orders a new series of bombing missions against Hanoi and other cities.

October 1972

Kissinger arranges a cease fire with North Vietnamese leaders. South Vietnamese president Thieu rejects the agreement.

November 1972

Nixon is reelected president by a wide margin.

January 1973

After stalled negotiations resume in Paris, all sides agree to accords that will end the war.

February 1973

North Vietnam begins returning American prisoners of war.

March 1973

All remaining U.S. combat troops are withdrawn from Vietnam. Only civilian aid and diplomatic personnel remain in Saigon.

August 1974

President Nixon resigns in order to avoid impeachment for his involvement in the

Watergate scandal. Vice President Gerald R. Ford takes office.

January 1975

North Vietnamese forces begin attacks against the South. The South Vietnamese forces fight a losing war. President Ford asks Congress for more aid to South Vietnam to stem the North Vietnamese tide, but he is refused.

April 1975

South Vietnamese president Thieu resigns after claiming he has been betrayed by American promises of support. Victorious North Vietnamese forces swarm into Saigon. Most of the remaining U.S. personnel in Vietnam are airlifted out of the fallen capital.

★ Index ★

★ Picture Credits ★

★ About the Editor ★

Author David M. Haugen edits books for Lucent Books and Greenhaven Press. He holds a master's degree in English literature ans has also worked as a writer and instructor.